# Dangerous Secrets

# Dangerous Secrets

## MALADAPTIVE RESPONSES TO STRESS

Michael P. Weissberg, M.D.

W · W · NORTON & COMPANY
*New York   London*

Copyright © 1983 by Michael P. Weissberg

All rights reserved.

Published simultaneously in Canada by George J. McLeod Limited, Toronto.

Printed in the United Sates of America.

The text of this book is composed in Baskerville, with display type set in Baker Signet. Composition and manufacturing by The Maple-Vail Book Manufacturing Group. Book design by A. Christopher Simon.

First Edition

Library of Congress Cataloging in Publication Data

Weissberg, Michael P.
  Dangerous secrets.

  Bibliography: p.
  Includes index.
  1. Mental illness—Etiology.  2. Stress (Psychology)
I. Title.  II. Title: Maladaptive response to stress.
RC455.4.S87W44  1983      616.85'82      82-24662

ISBN 0-393-01732-X

W. W. Norton & Company, Inc., 500 Fifth Avenue, New York, N.Y. 10110
W. W. Norton & Company Ltd., 37 Great Russell Street, London WC1B 3NU

1 2 3 4 5 6 7 8 9 0

*For C.C.*

# Contents

# Foreword

There is a persistent myth that dangerous behaviors occur only among certain segments of our society. We prefer to think that others, "elsewhere," are alcoholics or child abusers; people we know do not commit incest, abuse a spouse, or attempt suicide. The truth is that each of us, knowingly or not, will at some time have intimate contact with persons who have lost control of themselves and are acting in maladaptive, destructive ways. These people may be friends, family members, patients—or even oneself.

For the most part, we are more adept at dealing with physical distress than with psychological upset. Many of us do not recognize the early symptoms of behavioral problems or do not know what to do when dangerous behaviors are suspected or identified. This book attempts to answer frequently unspoken questions. In an authoritative way, it offers information that will be useful to family, friends, and health care professionals—in other words, to all of us who deal with the vagaries of human behavior.

Dr. Weissberg provides an excellent framework for an understanding of why people do what they do to each other and to themselves. Stress is an essential part of life, and we all respond to stress in diverse ways that are sometimes adaptive, sometimes not. Fortunately, poor responses to stress can often be understood and ameliorated if handled appropriately and at an early stage. But there are other instances when an understanding of why people neglect and abuse each other and their children, drink to excess, or kill themselves is not readily gained. Complex factors, woven into the life fabric, are involved. We know that people as adults tend to repeat what they experienced or witnessed when they were young. Yet as Dr. Weissberg notes, not all people raised in abusive and neglectful environments succumb to destructive behaviors in adulthood. This issue of stress resistance is one of the more fascinating and promising topics of contemporary behavioral research.

Dr. Weissberg also dispels the myth that the health care delivery system is uniformly well-equipped to recognize and treat destructive behaviors. There are many excellent people working in the health and mental health fields, but some professionals are not sufficiently trained to diagnose and treat dangerous behaviors in the most appropriate fashion. Along with the general public, these care-givers tend to minimize the existence of the problems, finding them frightening to uncover and deal with.

The understandable anxiety created by maladaptive responses to stress can be translated into a useful diagnostic and treatment tool if the anxiety is recognized and accepted. Preconscious, back-of-the-mind experiences with people may be an early warning signal that something is wrong. Observer discomfort can then become the impetus for further exploration rather than the cause for looking away. Dr. Weissberg discusses how health care providers—and the general public—can approach difficult problems, what the *early* clues are, and what action to take if someone is in trouble. His advice about how to evaluate the types of emergency medical and psychotherapeutic care offered to people involved in dangerous behavior, about what constitutes adequate care, and about what should be expected from providers are important contributions of this book.

10

Since 1974, Dr. Weissberg has been director of a nationally recognized training program in emergency psychiatry at the University of Colorado School of Medicine. He is coauthor of the acclaimed text *Clinical Psychiatry in Primary Care* and is actively involved in interdisciplinary psychiatric education. His extensive clinical experience is reflected in the case material he presents and in his lucid explanations of difficult clinical concepts. The story of Hansel and Gretel as recounted here vividly highlights certain aspects of the stress response and illustrates the problems of child abuse. The devastating impact of incest is poignantly described through the poem of a victim.

The information, insights, and perceptions contained in this book should become part of everyone's education. Only if this is accomplished will the people affected by these tragic human problems receive the attention and care they need.

HERBERT PARDES, M.D.
*Director, National Institute of Mental Health*

# Introduction

This book is about people who seem, at first glance, to be functioning well but are not; and about others whose problems, though obvious, are not fully appreciated. Dangerous behaviors are ubiquitous and can affect everyone. Those most frequently encountered are child abuse, incest, spouse abuse, and suicide. Because of its intimate association with the other dangerous behaviors, alcoholism must also be included.

My purpose is to increase understanding of these problems so that constructive responses can replace well-meaning but bewildered interventions or, as is often the case, harmful inaction. Dangerous behaviors do not occur "out of the blue." Yet many physicians, some psychotherapists, and the majority of lay people are not as knowledgeable about these problems as they should be. Lack of information, the covert nature of some behaviors, and the presence of observer anxiety often interfere with the realistic appraisal of people in trouble, whose problems then get out of hand. When the behaviors finally reach crisis proportion, it is clear that warning signals have existed for some time, indeed a lifetime.

In thinking back over my career as a psychiatrist, I have wondered how many times I overlooked or minimized the presence of dangerous behaviors. I can recall situations—both professional and personal—that at the time were ignored or rationalized, but that later became understandable. Nearly every day now, a new instance of unsuspected abuse, alcoholism, or suicidal intent is brought to my attention, either in my clinical practice, among the cases I supervise, or by colleagues with whom I consult. This happens so often that I am no longer surprised.

The ideas and observations presented here are those I have found most useful during my years of practice. The book is designed to provide the reader—both professional and non-professional—with a feel for identifying the dangerous behaviors and for helping people in trouble. The first chapter describes how stress can cause all of us to react in maladaptive and destructive ways, the early clues that can alert observers, and why those clues are usually overlooked. Chapters 2 to 6, devoted to specific syndromes, are organized to make information accessible and to "train" the reader in observation and effective interventions. Sections in each of the middle chapters are further subdivided to address three groups—family and friends, medical and health personnel, and psychiatric practitioners—so that these groups can gain awareness of the most helpful strategies (and the least, since they are so often utilized).

The last chapter, "Psychotherapy: Some Guidelines and Pitfalls," contains the essence of my ideas about what constitutes good psychiatric care. This chapter, for both the practitioner and the nonprofessional, is designed so that patients and their families can become more sophisticated consumers of health care, and so that clinicians can become more effective psychotherapists. Instances of adequate and suboptimal care are explored. People involved in dangerous behaviors often have a history of mistreatment. For this reason, and because of the special feelings these patients can arouse in practitioners, examples of abuse of the therapeutic situation are also presented.

This book is not meant to be an academically balanced text. I have written it from the vantage point of a psychodynamically oriented psychiatrist. Necessarily, I have adopted certain points of view to the relative exclusion of others. Psychodynamic thought is more heavily relied on, for instance, than learning theory, not because I discount the latter but because I find the former more compelling. Where appropriate, biologic, genetic, social, or other influences are taken into account. Some of the things I say are based on solid evidence, others on more speculative theorizing. All of the cases are authentic and internally consistent but have been disguised to protect the patient's true identity.

My interest in dangerous behaviors can be traced to certain key people. When Dr. Stuart Asch at The Mount Sinai Hospital in New York suggested that a patient of mine might have killed her child, I was incredulous. I now think he was correct. When I moved to the Colorado Psychiatric Hospital at the University of Colorado, where I became director of the Emergency Psychiatric Service, one of my first private patients was a middle class woman who was an abusive parent. I had my hands full and would have failed except for the help of Drs. Carl Pollock and Brandt Steele, experienced teachers and clinicians. Dr. Steele has continued to be a source of guidance and inspiration.

Many of my ideas were stimulated and sharpened during discussions with Dr. Claudia A. Carroll of the C. Henry Kempe National Center for the Prevention and Treatment of Child Abuse and Neglect. Her comments and suggestions about the manuscript were invaluable. Dr. Charlotte Weissberg, in providing me with other perspectives and points of view and in reviewing early drafts of the manuscript, has also been a helpful critic.

This book would not have been written without the initial encouragement of Helen Hans and Martha Saxton, both friends of long standing. Carol Houck Smith, my editor at Norton, has kept me on course with her firm and patient advice. Cindy Keck provided early help with preparation of the manuscript, but absolutely nothing would have been accomplished without the steady help of Nancy Olbricht and

Opal Every. On many Monday mornings, they politely hid their true feelings when I appeared with yet another revision.

Finally, a word of thanks to my many friends who put up with me since I decided to write this book.

MICHAEL P. WEISSBERG, M.D.

*November 1982*

# Dangerous Secrets

# 1

# Dangerous Behavior
## THE MALADAPTIVE RESPONSE

### THE PROBLEM

Many people cope with stress in maladaptive and dangerous ways. When pressures feel extreme, they lose control and resort to destructive behaviors in abortive attempts to reestablish mastery over themselves and their environment. The victims of such behaviors can be perpetrators in their own right. Alcoholism, child abuse, incest, spousal violence, and suicide are prime examples of maladaptive responses to stress. These behaviors cause severe harm to both victims and perpetrators and deeply affect family, friends, and clinicians.

People in trouble frequently do not appreciate the magnitude of their difficulties; if they do, they and their families generally feel such shame that they keep their problems secret. Overt and covert clues are ignored or overlooked, thus increasing the danger of permanent physical and psychological damage to the victim, perpetrator, and family. Dangerous behaviors usually remain under cover until events occur that can no longer be rationalized. Even then the problem may be minimized, and opportunities for help undermined and missed.

Although each of the dangerous behaviors above is a dis-

19

tinct problem, they have much in common, often overlap, and involve similar responses and issues for family, friends, and clinicians. When such troubles are finally "discovered," people are needlessly surprised, since in retrospect it is clear that trouble existed for months or even years. The clues are usually obvious. For example, in the following cases, the true meaning of accidents, repetitive suicidal behavior, and childhood trauma was not recognized:

A young psychologist began drinking heavily in college. This continued through graduate school, and although the woman's friends and husband knew about her difficulty, they did little to help. Later her children began having difficulties at school, and the mother lost her driver's license because of repeated "accidents." During one Christmas holiday she fell and fractured her arm. While recuperating she began to see snakes and thought she was being attacked by various animals. She convinced her husband to buy her a bottle to help with her "nerves." The woman subsequently died of cirrhosis of the liver.

A seventeen-year-old honors student was brought to her physician following an "accidental" overdose of sleeping pills. Both parents seemed very concerned and were reluctant to leave her alone with the physician. When interviewed alone, the patient hinted at vague difficulties at home, but the nature of the difficulties was not fully determined. Following another overdose attempt it was learned that the patient's father had been sexually molesting her for years. This also explained why the patient's parents had hovered at her side during the first visit to the physician.

A doctor's wife brought her daughter to an orthopedist because of a sprained ankle. Because the child was unable to put weight on the leg, X-rays were taken that revealed a fracture. Seven months later, the child was seen by another doctor because of another broken bone. The possibility of abuse was not suspected, because this was a doctor's child. Only after a third fracture occurred two months later was the family properly evaluated. The mother then admitted throwing the child against the wall in order to "discipline" her. The father maintained that he knew nothing of these difficulties.

People in trouble feel trapped by their circumstances and personal histories; they view themselves as helpless to effect positive, healthy changes in their lives, and this pessimistic outlook, although not warranted, can become a self-fulfilling prophecy. When these people are ignored, they remain isolated and maladaptive behaviors persist. However, with knowledgeable and helpful intervention, chances for a less destructive outcome can be improved. People in trouble want to be found out but usually cannot speak directly about their difficulties. In a written confession, a man who was having intercourse with his daughter for over three years had this to say:

I don't know how it got out of hand but my wife and I were having problems and I felt unwanted and unneeded. I felt so miserable—I don't know how it happened—I turned to my daughter. I hated myself—*I wanted to tell someone, but I was too ashamed,* I don't really know how I could have done such a thing but I did have sex with her. (*Emphasis added*)

One-half of American families in *all social groups* will, at some time, become involved in a dangerous behavior; one-eighth of all couples will engage in severe violence. If this isn't surprising, the following is. In one study, a third of college students reported a history of sexual molestation during childhood. The incidence of incest is now thought to be 200,000 cases a year. At least 500,000 children are physically abused annually; countless more are emotionally neglected.

21

(This less obvious and more subtle emotional neglect is the true pathogenic agent in abuse and causes the long-term psychological damage.) Suicide at 25,000 cases per year is surely a low estimate. Ten times that many people are known to make attempts. In fact, suicide is a leading cause of death in young adults, and when combined with homicide and accidents, violence becomes *the* leading cause of death in this young age group.

Drinking is closely associated with maladaptive behaviors. Alcohol "heats up" the atmosphere and acts as a catalyst for all kinds of destructive activity. Over sixty percent of all homicides involve alcohol, as do twenty to fifty percent of all cases of incest, child abuse, spouse abuse, and suicide. The victim *and* perpetrator are often intoxicated in spouse abuse and homicide. And ten percent of all Americans drink enough to be classified as problem drinkers—another fact that, like many others, is often ignored and underestimated.

Is the incidence of maladaptive activity increasing or does improved reporting explain what appears to be a rise in dangerous behavior? Probably both are true. It may (or may not) be a comfort to realize that these five problems are not recently invented—they have long histories and are found in most societies, sometimes supported by the culture, sometimes not. The Crusades, the Inquisition, the Nazi holocaust represent concentrated and notorious examples of cultural support. The Bible, folk tales, myths, nursery rhymes, and examples of art all contain ample evidence that dangerous behaviors have occupied the minds of every generation. Shakespeare's works are full of aggression gone awry. Alcoholism, family violence, incest, and suicide were well represented by the Elizabethans as they were by the Greeks. These things have always been with us; the modern world does not have the corner on maladaptive responses to stress.

We are currently preoccupied with violence that happens elsewhere. The ready availability of information disseminated by the media has created a mind-set that expects catastrophe; when violence occurs many miles away, people feel threatened. A murder randomly committed in New York frightens citizens in Ohio. This may account in part for the widespread and probably exaggerated conviction that we are experiencing an epidemic of dangerous behavior. Crime statistics, like any others, are subject to manipulation and differing interpretation. For example, the Uniform Crime Reports of the F.B.I. suggest that the per capita rate of violent crime tripled from 1960 to 1979. However, the Census Bureau gives another picture. Twice each year the Census Bureau interviews 132,000 people in 60,000 households about whether they were victimized, assaulted, robbed, and so forth. These victim surveys suggest that the rate of serious crime remained essentially unchanged between 1973 and 1979 (*New York Times,* 8 March 1981).

This book is about problems close to home. It is not about crime between strangers but about the dangerous behaviors that occur between family and friends. There are at least 50 million pistols in the U.S.; over 100 are sold daily in Denver alone. These weapons may be bought for "protection from the outside," but many are turned on people known to the gun owner. *The majority of truly dangerous, maladaptive behavior takes place in the home and between people who know each other, sometimes very well.* Everyone can respond to stress in maladaptive ways, and, with shadings along a continuum, all of us can find ourselves actively involved in dangerous behavior.

Although these behaviors seem senseless, they make sense once the participants' circumstances are known and histories uncovered. Abused or neglected children are likely to participate in spousal violence as adults. Abusive parents generally were abused when young, and alcoholism runs in families; one-third of problem drinkers are self-medicating an underlying psychological illness. Others turn to alcohol to deal with the discomfort of stressful situations. Incest is associated with certain predictable family dynamics. Suicide is viewed by suicidal people as the only solution to seemingly intolerable life events. Furthermore, all these behaviors involve the social system in which they occur. None happens in a vacuum; there are always survivors and other participants. Friends, family, and clinicians are part of the problem or become part of the solution; they too may experience maladaptive responses to people in trouble.

## The Family: Collusion, Denial, Guilt, and Silence

> If she isn't good enough for the family, then she just isn't good enough for anyone.
>
> *Old saying*

Maladaptive behaviors are self-perpetuating over generations. All may occur more frequently in certain families. Some families are primarily incestuous, others physically abusive, and still others alcoholic or suicidal. Chaotic families may be involved with all of these behaviors. Both nature and nurture are operating here. It is not uncommon to find multiple generational involvement in alcoholism, spousal violence, child abuse, incest, or suicide. Each family has its own culture, style, and way of doing things.

Home is not the safe place it is supposed to be. Family pathology directly contributes to the genesis of incest, child abuse, and spousal violence. Collusive silence and covert acquiescence contribute to these syndromes as well as to alcoholism and suicide. "Death wishes" frequently complicate suicidal crises. At times suicidal persons are even "dared" to commit the act. Guns, pills, or other means of death may be left lying about, clues to an unconscious antipathy toward the suicidal person. For instance, while on a visit home, the son of a physician asked his father about the best way to commit suicide. The father said alcohol and sleeping pills were most effective. A few days later the father sent his son a bottle of Chivas Regal as "a present." The boy used it in an unsuccessful overdose attempt two weeks later.

There are other examples of collusion. Alcohol is often

bought for a known alcoholic. The majority of "non-abusive" parents know that their spouse is beating their child. Mothers are frequently aware that their husbands are sexually molesting their daughters yet do nothing about it. Some mothers even seem covertly to promote such behavior: "Why don't you take care of each other while I am gone?" is taken, and meant, literally. Such collusion exists for diverse reasons but it is a common finding that members of families involved in maladaptive behaviors are often so mutually dependent and so frightened of being deserted that a tremendous amount of difficulty is tolerated in order to keep the family together.

These families experience cycles of denial and guilt; denial that anything is wrong or, if there is, that it won't happen again. But all of these behaviors are repetitive and symptomatic of underlying, long-standing difficulties. "He only beats me when he is drunk" means that it will happen again. Only when denial is overcome will help be sought.

Guilt also plagues most of these families. Sometimes the self-blame is a defense against anger at the dysfunctional family member. At other times, the guilt is an accurate reflection of the family's participation in the dangerous behavior; for example, for keeping things quiet. It is important, however, not to look for the "cause" of one person's destructive behavior in other members of the family. "Gas-lighting" rarely occurs; someone is unlikely to drive another "crazy." Although suicidal people blame others for their feelings, they are, at bottom, responsible for their own lives. Incestuous fathers frequently point to their wives' lack of affection as the "cause" of their incestuous activity. Abusive mothers blame their child's misbehavior for their own. Knowing, and keeping clear, who is doing what and to whom is extremely important since responsibility and role definitions tend to be vague in these families; mutual recrimination is a commonly used defense. The defense of silence, however, does allow maladaptive responses to continue—and in this sense family and friends are responsible.

## Denial of Danger, Overlooking Dangerous Secrets

> People only see what they are
> prepared to see.
>
> *Ralph Waldo Emerson*

Dangerous behaviors promote anxiety; they are too stimulating for most of us to deal with. Anxiety and / or ignorance are also common reactions among health care professionals. They share the same sensibilities as the rest of the population; they don't want to find situations in their patients that are perceived as disgusting, frightening, evil, and out of control. Clinicians may ascribe to the mistaken notion that what they don't know, don't find, and don't diagnose will not hurt them.

This is extremely unfortunate since almost *all* the victims and perpetrators of these behaviors give multiple clues that they are in trouble—as if they want to be found out. For example, over half of the people who commit suicide visit their medical doctor in the month before they kill themselves; 80 percent of those who die of an overdose do so with one prescription that they have recently obtained. Suicidal people, like others with covert problems, provide ample but sometimes indirect clues. There are also many missed therapeutic opportunities in child abuse, often long before serious physical damage occurs. The doctor's child, previously mentioned, saw three different physicians (and countless friends and family members) for a series of major accidents before the possibility of child abuse was even considered. A young mother of two developed the classic symptoms of depression but obtained the means of suicide, sleeping pills, from her doctor. He did not adequately evaluate her for depression or suicidal tendencies. A lawyer's wife developed bruises and other difficulties during her pregnancy but spousal violence was missed by friends and overlooked by her obstetrician. They accepted her excuses and false explanations. She miscarried after being pushed down the stairs by her husband. A middle-aged

26

schoolteacher also had numerous "accidents," often had the "flu," and died in a fire caused by her lighted cigarette. She had been a severe alcoholic for years. The precocious thirteen-year-old daughter of an army sergeant repeatedly visited her family doctor because of a series of physical complaints including urinary tract infections. Her father always accompanied her to the doctor, who would reassure the father that his daughter was not sexually active. However, the father had been having intercourse with his daughter for years. This was revealed when the girl told a playmate who then told her own mother.

Denial of trouble takes many forms. Clues are minimized, joked about, explained away, or called something else. Semantics plays a big part in minimizing what is actually occurring; euphemisms are employed to hide what is really going on. A "good" drinker, marital "disputes," or "stern disciplinarian" can mean alcoholism, spousal violence, or child abuse. Explanations of "minor accidents" are gratefully accepted to explain the bruises and broken bones of child or spouse abuse. The "flu" excuses drunken behavior.

If danger is recognized, it may be rationalized by superficial explanations. Danger is noticed but not appreciated for what it is: "They have problems only when he or she is high or drunk" or "It must be that time of the month" or "He must be having a bad day." Much destructive behavior occurs while the victim or perpetrator is drunk or around menses, when under stress or in response to "bad days." A patient may feel hopeless after a personal loss and let this be known in various ways. But family and friends may minimize lethality by saying: "Of course he feels bad, such and such just happened to him." These explanations defuse the need for alarm, as if the potential for danger could be decreased by providing an explanation of *why* something is happening. Explaining it as "just" a depression, a financial setback, or a "stage" in life misses the point. Such explanations are offered to minimize the danger, protect the observer, and not help people in trouble.

Prejudice is also a factor. Same-class bias interferes with the early identification of these problems in others. People don't want to see in people like themselves what may be present in themselves. The joke that doctors diagnose alcoholism only in those patients who drink more than they do makes this point. Assumptions that alcoholics are all skid-row bums are incorrect. This logic misses 95 percent of all problem drinkers, most of whom do not look like "alcoholics."

Other preconceptions determine whether danger will be recognized. People have strange and misleading ideas about participants in dangerous behavior. For example, if a doctor or cocktail waitress each leaves a young child home alone for long periods of time, which one would be more likely to be thought of as a neglectful parent? In truth, each is responding inadequately to the needs of a child. Yet explanations that the child is "mature" or "old for his age" will be more readily accepted from the physician.

Still other prejudices can prevail. Incest occurs only among the poor and illiterate; not among the educated and wealthy. Truck drivers, not doctors and lawyers, beat their wives. Women are always victims; men the aggressors. The biases are as endless as the missed opportunities for help. Prejudice clouds perceptions and the secrets remain underground.

Once dangerous behavior is finally recognized and its full impact realized, other rationalizations may come into play: "A man's home is his castle," or "Don't people have a right to fight, discipline their children, drink, or commit suicide?" All are interesting philosophical questions, but they are usually raised in order to decrease the anxiety of discovery and to remove any responsibility for action.

# THE SYMPTOMS OF TROUBLE
# THE CLUES TO DANGER

There can no great smoke arise, but
there must be some fire, no great
report, without great suspicion.

*John Lyly*

How does one know that someone is in trouble? No one symptom signifies involvement in dangerous, maladaptive activity per se, but there are symptoms that problems do exist. Such symptoms mean that the person is in flux, psychological homeostasis has been upset for some reason, and maladaptive attempts may be made to reestablish a sense of control.

During periods of high tension, people regress and resort to immature behavior. Reality sense is diminished. Cognition is adversely affected; judgment is altered, as is the capacity for abstract thought. Thinking becomes less flexible and more concrete, which causes a reduction in creativity and coping abilities. The psychological "horizon" is limited and perspective decreased, and a tendency toward action exists, thus increasing the danger. People become egocentric and impulsive and lose their altruistic attitude. Relationships are impaired. Preoccupied with themselves and their physical functioning, people may develop diverse physical symptoms.

Different stages of the stress response, although not always clearly demarcated, have distinct characteristics. This reaction may last minutes or years, but throughout people attempt to protect themselves from real or imagined threats (see diagram). The first phase, denial that anything is wrong, is followed by periods of disorganization and symptom formation. The anxiety and depression and other symptoms of this stage signal that psychological homeostasis has been interrupted. Various attempts to retain equilibrium are then tried—some adaptive, others not—followed by the end of the crisis situation. For example, a man who finds he has locked the keys in

29

## THE STRESS RESPONSE

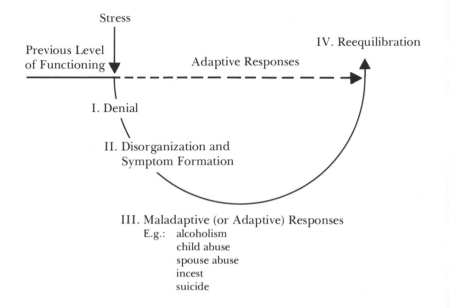

Stress

Previous Level
of Functioning

Adaptive Responses

IV. Reequilibration

I. Denial

II. Disorganization and
Symptom Formation

III. Maladaptive (or Adaptive) Responses
E.g.:  alcoholism
child abuse
spouse abuse
incest
suicide

his car may make a frantic search of his pockets, even though it is clear that the keys are in the car and that the second set is at home. This denial may be replaced by anxiety and symptom formation until other maneuvers are considered. Kicking the car or smashing the windshield would be maladaptive, misguided attempts to undo the upset of the crisis, while returning home for a second set of keys could be considered a more appropriate response.

Anything that is felt as a threat to well-being can provoke dangerous and maladaptive behavior. But before people resort to maladaptive responses—as with the man and his lost keys—they usually experience periods of mounting tension and symptom formation. These symptoms of the build-up phase form the early clues to potential problems. They are like a fever—they are *general* clues to an underlying disorder. Only after examining the situation can a judgment be reached as to where the person really is in the stress response.

The symptoms of mounting tension are variable and involve multiple behavioral, psychological, and somatic changes—many of which are mediated via the autonomic nervous system and hormonal pathways. The degree of personal alteration depends on the nature of the stress; on its intensity and chronicity, its psychological meaning and how resistant the individual is to the stimulus. Shifts in functioning are not always readily apparent. Alterations may be minor and subtle. Even substantial changes may be overlooked and dismissed as being "due to weather," "something eaten," or "just one of those days." Often people in trouble are not aware of what is bothering them—only that they feel tense, out of sorts, and uneasy.

Many of these changes can, of course, have basis in physical and organic pathology. The possible presence of physical disease should not be overlooked and medical attention should be sought if symptoms persist or worsen. Although stress increases the likelihood of some medical illnesses, physical illness often contributes to impulsive, destructive behaviors either by acting as a psychological stressor or by directly interfering with mental functioning.

For purposes of clarity, the following clues to the presence of stress have been divided into somatic, behavioral, and psychological alterations. Simply put, *any change in any sphere of functioning* is a clue to stress and is cause for further examination. Attempts should be made to understand *why* the change has occurred; what has "upset the apple cart" and what the potential for danger actually is.

SOME COMMON INDICATORS OF TENSION

*Somatic*

Palpitations, sweating, dry mouth
Frequent urination
Changes in eating and sleep patterns, either increased or decreased
Bruxism (nocturnal teeth grinding)
Fatigue and malaise

Migraine and other head pain
Gastrointestinal disturbances, vomiting, diarrhea
Back and other musculoskeletal pain
Change in menses

*Behavioral*

Restlessness, irritability, hyperactivity, troubled sleep
Aggressive behavior—increase in fights, arguments, trouble with the law, and so forth
Impulsive behavior
Accident proneness
Increased drug taking: alcohol, tobacco, sedative-hypnotics, and so forth
Increased visits to physicians, emergency rooms, clinics, with real and imagined physical complaints

*Psychological*

Anxiety, depression, emotional lability
Numbing anhedonia (no capacity for enjoyment)
Startle reactions
Phobias and other anxiety symptoms
Hypnoid, dissociative, or other bizarre states of consciousness
Nightmares; intrusive anxiety-producing thoughts
Problems with concentration and memory
Worsening of preexisting psychiatric problems

Symptoms of stress in children and adolescents differ somewhat from those in adults. Children and adolescents usually have lower frustration tolerances and are more likely to act rather than to allow themselves to feel or experience. Therefore, behavioral disorders frequently mask depressions in the young. Truancy, drug taking, alcohol abuse, antisocial or suicidal behaviors are often indications of underlying problems that may be both the result and cause of dangerous behavior. For example, runaway behavior, truancy, and suicidal activity are frequently found among female adolescent victims of incest and are known as the Incest Triad. Adolescent alcoholism can also be a clue to physical abuse. Bedwetting, tantrums, school problems, and eating difficulties in children can be indicators of family pathology, spousal violence, child abuse, incest, and so forth. Therefore, *every* behavioral alteration should be examined as if it were symptomatic of other, potentially lethal difficulties. A juvenile delinquent may be described as a "crook," a "hood," and "evil" and also be a depressed, abused, and suicidal child.

## Accidents and Somatic Complaints

Accidents and somatic complaints deserve more complete mention: accidents because they are frequently overlooked markers of stress and somatic complaints because their importance is usually ignored by friends, family, and physicians.

The combination of accidents, suicide, and homicide is the third leading cause of death in the United States and the *first* cause among people under age 39. While other causes of death in young adults are declining, the overall death rate is increasing due to these dangerous behaviors. Many accidents are, in fact, intentional, the result of suicidal and homicidal behavior. Others are due to unconscious factors: accident "proneness" is often the result of psychological disequilibrium.

True accidents do occur, but it is always useful to examine their circumstances and psychological context in order to uncover less accidental contributing factors. Voltaire's notion that there is no such thing as an accident may be extreme, but is clinically useful, as can be seen in the following situation:

A twenty-six-year-old machinist visited various medical emergency rooms twenty-three times over a two-and-a-half-year period. He had numerous accidents at work, complained of headaches, numbness, back spasms, problems with sleep, and weight loss. It was found out later that his visits began when his wife became pregnant. Finally, when his child was eighteen months old, it was discovered that he had been beating his wife and

33

was terrified of doing the same to his child. He said, "I think I am accident prone. There are more ways to kill yourself than to commit suicide." He also said that he drank heavily and "that may be another way to destroy myself." When his childhood medical charts were reviewed, he was found to have a past history of many emergency room visits for trauma, cuts, and bruises that probably were inflicted by his mother and stepfather. These clues to child abuse were missed when the patient was young.

This man experienced true accidents but used the excuse of accidents to cover up nonaccidental trauma and also developed multiple somatic complaints as symptoms of distress. A victim of severe childhood abuse, he was later involved in spousal violence, alcoholism, potential child abuse, and covert suicidal behavior.

Such people place themselves in situations where accidents are much more likely to occur than would normally. Accidents then are no longer accidental; rather, they are the result of unconscious action. Risky behavior occurs in response to life stresses, probably in a misguided, unconscious attempt to master anxiety, to tempt fate, to seek punishment for some unknown transgressions, or because of a loss of the will to live. For example:

One year after his wife left him for another man, an accomplished mountaineer was killed in an avalanche. He needlessly exposed himself to high-risk conditions while crossing an avalanche chute. He could have gone around this obstacle with little difficulty. Two months earlier, he had narrowly missed serious injury during an ice climbing accident. His behavior had changed during the last year of his life. His habits were more erratic, he seemed tense and depressed, and his work performance had substantially declined.

Physical factors also complicate the occurrence of accidents. Drugs and alcohol are intimately involved here, as well as differences in gender. For example, premenstrual tension is associated with accidents in women, as well as with other impulsive, aggressive behaviors—the highest risk time for accidents among women seems to be the four days preceding menstruation and menses proper. Thus, with accidents, there are multiple psychological and physiological factors involved, in addition to the play of chance.

An increase in body awareness and in physical concerns usually accompanies periods of tension and psychological turmoil. The tension may subside and symptoms disappear after the person resorts to action (abuse or drinking, for example), only to recur when a new crisis arises. Frequently, these physical complaints can serve as a covert plea for help when patients seek attention for physical ills. Unfortunately, these patients offer little direct information about what is going on and physicians usually don't ask. For example:

A young nurse sought medical attention for head and neck pains of recent onset. She was given a number of drugs, including narcotics and tranquilizers, which she used in an overdose attempt. Only then was it learned that she had been brutally assaulted and raped shortly before the onset of her symptoms. She had told no one about the attack, since she was so intensely ashamed about what had happened.

This is not a minor point. People react with their bodies; their symptoms are clear indications of personal distress. In the month before they die, over half of the people who kill themselves visit their medical doctors with various vague physical complaints. Victims *and* perpetrators of spousal violence, child abuse, and incest visit hospitals and clinics with various complaints not only directly attributable to physical trauma but also to anxiety and depression. Alcoholics fre-

35

quently present a panoply of vague ailments, particularly those referable to the gastrointestinal tract.

Physicians find these patients frustrating, since most of the ills cannot be "cured" without taking the patient's psychosocial situation into consideration. Unfortunately, labels such as Crock, Turkey, GOMER (Get Out Of My Emergency Room), WADAO (Weak And Dizzy All Over), and other disparagements have been used to describe these patients. This creates another conceptual hurdle that has to be overcome in order to identify people in trouble. Vague and persistent complaints usually create feelings of helplessness in the observer. However, if they are recognized for what they sometimes are—clues to psychological distress rather than physical problems—proper care can be administered.

## THE CAUSES OF DANGEROUS
## BEHAVIORS

It is an illusion to think that we can know exactly why people do what they do when they do it. Superficial explanations are usually invoked to allay observer anxiety. The mechanisms for dangerous behaviors are complex, but there are relevant findings that are applicable to all, as well as to each specific syndrome. With physical illness it is impossible to say who will develop pneumonia, but one can point to the person at greater risk. The same can be done with maladaptive behaviors.

There are both predispositions to behavior and precipitating causes for behavior. Events can be described along varying axes. For example, genetics plays an important if not fully understood role. A biologically active or difficult child can be the crucial factor in precipitating child abuse if the parents are marginally adjusted. Alcoholism has a genetic component. Chance certainly is another element. The presence of a weapon frequently turns a violent impulse into a suicide or murder. Alcohol, or any other substance that affects the ability to reason and reduces normally expected mental capabilities makes impulsive behavior more likely.

Physical disease plays a part. The risk of maladaptive responses increases as the ability to think declines. For example, Huntington's chorea drastically altered the quality of one child's upbringing, changing a mother into a dangerous woman. Woody Guthrie, in *Bound for Glory*, described his mother as "all right for a time" until something took her over. She would turn into another person, twitch and snarl at her children. She turned into something "terrible." In this case, the presence of a physical disease precipitated a potentially abusive situation.

The fragmentation of social groups and the decline of the extended family and therefore of mutual social supports have a definite effect on the ability to tolerate stress. An adequate social system helps to absorb tension and decreases the chances of dangerous behavior. However, the presence of an adequate social system depends, in part, on an adequate upbringing. People who were neglected as children tend to be isolated as adults. Certainly, someone who never was able to rely on parents while growing up will have difficulty turning to others for help. It is also easier to be rich. A wealthy family under stress is better off than a poor one; even so, both may be in jeopardy.

Although people are not sponges, indiscriminately soaking up what they are exposed to, the influence of television and violent games should not be underestimated. No doubt sadistic, maladaptive and dangerous ways of acting can, in part, be learned. In a way, television represents the dual attributes of the childhood emotional neglect and overstimulation so often experienced by people in trouble. Parents abrogate parental functions to the television set; human conversation and interaction are replaced by passive watching of an electronic object, with the result that children are overstimulated. The average preschool child watches over fifty hours of television per week—more than seven hours each day. Between the ages of five and fifteen children will see more than thirteen thousand people killed on television. However, despite the potentially awesome influence of TV, what is observed in the home has a greater impact on later development.

There may be phylogenetic influences on maladaptive behavior. Primate research indicates that certain mechanisms involved in child abuse, for example, may not be unique to humans. Aberrations in the early social environment of primates can create aggressive behavior in adult primates. Research suggests that social isolation, environmental stressors, and a history of early abuse can lead to abusive parents both in primates and in man. Thus, factors found in humans may, in part, be phylogenetically determined.

Whether maladaptive behaviors are innate or acquired—they are probably both—is an important and interesting question. But if what is meant by this question is whether they can be made to disappear, then it is naïve. Behavior is complex, and if one "cause" diminishes, another takes its place. The combinations and permutations are endless. More often than not, people involved in dangerous behaviors are bound to repeat what they witnessed or experienced in the past; their adaptive maneuvers are most heavily influenced by their histories.

When faced with stress, people tend to act predictably and consistently. Repetition and constancy of response are part of one's "character," which in turn is a function of nature and nurture. Some people are adaptable and can alter their behavior to meet the requirements of the present. Others are stereotyped, responding in more rigid and less creative ways. The latter group is responding more to past experiences than to present circumstances, and the potential for danger increases with this loss of flexibility. Just as some people react to stress with their gastrointestinal tract and others with changes in sexual functioning, in appetite, or in sleep patterns, others will respond with violence or other destructive behaviors.

## Maladaptive Responses
## and Stress Tolerance

Stress is anything perceived as dangerous. It contains within it a threat to security and self-esteem; it precipitates fears of loss or failure. The source of stress may be major, such as the death of a parent or spouse, or as minor as a broken television to an overwhelmed mother who uses the set as an electronic babysitter. It may be privately perceived, of significance to one individual, or an overwhelming event that affects everyone, such as the development of a physical illness, a natural disaster, or a change in financial circumstances. Success— which is frequently accompanied by fears of failure, among other anxieties—can be unsettling. A job promotion or graduation may be too much for some people to handle.

Other major life events can precipitate crises and evoke maladaptive responses. Pregnancy is a time of high risk for both incest and spousal violence. The loss of a job, relative, or personal self-esteem may evoke violent action, a drinking bout, or suicide. Threats of loss or fears of humiliation are important. Past losses can be a factor in the genesis of all the dangerous behaviors. The threatened loss of a mate frequently precipitates spousal violence or incest.

In folklore, the story of Hansel and Gretel is a striking example of dangerous behavior—child neglect—precipitated by a maladaptive response to the crisis of potential starvation. Hansel and Gretel were the children of a poor woodcutter and his wife. When famine struck the land and the father could no longer feed the family, he posed the problem to his wife: "What is to become of us? How are we to feed our poor children when we have nothing for ourselves?" The mother devised a plan to take the children deep into the forest and abandon them there, each with only a piece of bread. "They won't be able to find their way back, and so we shall be rid of them."

The tale illustrates how child mistreatment resulted from stress, parental egocentricity, and an inability to maintain an

39

empathic parental attitude. Collusion is also well illustrated by the father's acquiescence to the mother's murderous plans. As we know, Hansel and Gretel were sent into the forest to fend for themselves and to die. Luckily, they were more resourceful and adaptive than their parents. After a few false starts, they were able to make their way to safety.

All of us attempt to undo the threat to physical safety and psychological well-being that stress precipitates. Reactions can range from creative and adaptive planning all the way to drastic, destructive action. Let us suppose that someone driving to work is cut off by another car. One person might feel annoyed but make a joke or ignore the provocation. Others might curse or make various well-known hand gestures, particularly if they felt humiliated or offended. Still others would speed up, tailgate, and perhaps try to retake the lead. A small percentage of people would precipitate a physical confrontation. Fortunately, an even smaller percentage of people would attempt to kill the other driver. Such deaths, while rare, do occur.

Certain factors make the loss of control more likely and have the effect of "releasing" maladaptive behaviors. Prior stresses, a bad night's sleep, or anything else that adversely affects cognition and self-control are important. Alcohol lubricates destructive responses. The presence of a provocative victim or a weapon can transform an argument into a homicide. Even the weather plays a part; cabin fever results in increased depression and alcoholism. Heavy, persistent winds are said to increase irritability and impulsive behavior.

There are clear physiological components to stress tolerance as well. As mentioned, women are much more likely to be involved in accidents during menses and the four days before than at other times during the menstrual cycle. During this time women are also much more likely to be involved in violent crime and aggressive outbursts. One study indicated that about half of crimes committed by women occurred during this premenstrual and menstrual period. Physiological changes are stressful in themselves and further weaken the organism's ability to deal with other tensions.

The ability to tolerate stress also depends, in large part, on how well the mechanisms of self-control have been internalized and on the reservoir of self-esteem that has been developed through early upbringing. There is a broad range of "good enough" parenting, and children who feel secure about themselves and their place in the world are unlikely to resort to maladaptive behaviors.

However, childhood overstimulation and neglect often lead to the development of a poor and incomplete sense of self and, consequently, to inadequate self-regulatory mechanisms. As adults, people who have had such childhoods are easily threatened and quickly resort to destructive action. They were flooded with feelings as children, being both overstimulated and unprotected by their parents. Some were sexually or physically abused or witnessed abuse and violence. As adults, they act quickly and, at times, destructively, to prevent psychic overload; they lack the internal emotional elasticity necessary to deal effectively with stress. Stress tolerance, then, depends on a warm, praising family; healthy, positive relationships with parents lead to greater emotional resiliency. Children must experience the protective shield of adequate parenting so that they can make this shield part of themselves when they grow older.

Physical abuse in children is easy to spot because of the trauma and bruises; emotional neglect is more difficult to identify. Yet such neglect may be even more damaging. Children, for example, may be sent to camp or boarding school at too early an age, thus being forced inappropriately to rely on themselves. Other examples of such nonempathic parenting are the "latch-key kids" who come home from school to an empty house with a door key around their necks. While this is not always bad, it can be indicative of emotional neglect. Many parents do not view their children as children at all but treat them as siblings or as adults. At times children are even forced to care for their parents. This defect in parental stance is not always easily noted and examples of such inadequate parenting can be quite subtle.

Children at risk, even when they do not directly experience

or witness violence, do not develop a sense of certainty about their environment and lack a sense of security about their place in the world. They grow independent prematurely, since they must learn to rely on themselves and not their parents. One child, a daughter of an alcoholic, said that she was "old by the time I was five." Brittle pseudomaturity replaces healthy development. Underneath this facade these children are extremely dependent, isolated, lonely, and easily humiliated. They are easily stressed.

Inconsistent parenting, which can lead to defective development, is often characterized by alternating periods of overstimulation and neglect. While this may be obvious in overtly disorganized families, it may be overlooked if the family seems otherwise to be intact. For example:

A boy of three was left alone asleep outside in a car on a cold winter evening while his parents visited some friends. The parents seemed unconcerned. When at the insistence of the hostess he was finally brought in, the mother lifted her floor-length skirt, and the boy spent the next ten minutes sheltered under it, with his face in her lap.

The parents, professional people, were not aware of their pattern of alternating neglect and overstimulation. They did not consider that the boy may have been frightened and cold in the car or that the overstimulation of such intimacy under her skirt was equally inappropriate.

Unfortunately, inadequate parenting is much more widespread than was once thought. A significant number of "normal" mothers simply do not like their children. And unloved children are more likely than others to grow up to be unloving, insecure, and emotionally brittle adults.

On the other hand, some people seem to be stress-"resistant" even though they may have experienced chaotic upbringings. The reasons for this are not clear, but it may be that an attenuated, well-timed adversity can strengthen character. Many such people also form significant long-term relationships with other nurturant figures in their environment (grandparents, siblings) if their parents are functionally or actually unavailable. Biological factors must also play a role. Some babies are sturdier than others; some children can bring out the best in any adult, thus getting the most out of their environments. And some people are "self-righting," landing on their feet no matter what the past or present provocation.

Early developmental histories do not *predict* the later outcome for children; early experiences make things possible, not inevitable. Why people resort to maladaptive responses when under stress is a highly complex and personal issue. However, it is safe to say that the ability to adapt to stress is associated with childhood experiences, the development of a sense of security and self-esteem and the availability of empathic parental figures early in life.

## Characteristics of Dangerous Behavior: Egocentricity and Repetition

Egocentricity is a characteristic of people involved in maladaptive behaviors. They think of themselves first; they are unable to empathize accurately. Often they cannot gauge their effect on others. For example, a new mother was found slapping her day-old infant because he was "asleep" and not "paying attention" to her. Another mother left her daughter with a mannequin "for company" when she went out. Some people are always this self-centered, others less so. Hansel and Gretel's mother abandoned her children because she was hungry. Another mother put her children to sleep when she, herself, was tired. This deficit in empathic understanding makes further dangerous behavior that much more possible.

People in trouble are often convinced of the correctness of what they do. They feel they have a right to pursue the car that cuts them off or to attack the person who humiliates them. Their drinking is not a problem; they have a right to beat a child or spouse, to sexually molest a child. They feel that suicide is the only reasonable alternative.

This egocentricity is related to deficits in reality testing.

43

Often these people grew up in environments where they were exposed to similar behavior. In fact, many fail to realize that they were abused and neglected as children, since this activity was considered a "normal" part of their upbringing. When as adults they repeat what they learned as children, they have a hard time thinking anything is wrong. This distortion of reality can reach extreme proportions even when such people might not be considered impaired in other areas:

A shy and intelligent lawyer was involved in spousal violence that led to his wife's miscarriage. He denied having been abused as a child yet described an extremely violent childhood. His father would hit him with belts and his fists, often leaving welts and bruises. His father stopped this when his son threatened him with a baseball bat. "But," the son said, "I wasn't abused, I deserved every beating I got."

Another example of distorted perception was overheard at a dinner party:

"I am very close to my family. They were always very demonstrative and loving. When I disagreed with my mother she threw whatever was nearest at hand at me. Once it happened to be a knife and I needed ten stitches in my leg. A few years later my father tried to choke me when I began dating a boy he didn't like. They really are very concerned about me."

Maladaptive behaviors are repetitive. Overstimulated children frequently crave overstimulation as adults. They may seek this in chaotic relationships, through drugs and alcohol, or by participation in other dangerous activities, such as high-risk sports. One abused child became a compulsive rock climber. He had the recurrent fantasy of the "final climb"; of completing an impossible climb, without protection, and then falling back into space to be smashed on the rocks below.

THE MALADAPTIVE RESPONSE

Such people try to recreate and therefore unconsciously maintain their old, usually parental, relationships. They confuse overstimulation and neglect with love. They recreate in the present those older patterns of the past. Consequently, they may involve themselves in a series of relationships, all of a (self-)destructive nature. The uninformed may ascribe such repetitive behavior to "bad luck"—not to the insight that people constantly create new editions of old stories.

Aside from wishing to maintain high levels of excitement, there may be an attempt to master memories of past situations when a child felt helpless, victimized, or out of control. The child-victim becomes the adult-aggressor. Identifying with the aggressor, becoming like the violent parent, magically decreases the anxiety of earlier victimization. Children who witnessed incest or were victims themselves may become incestuous parents. At times adults play both roles and damage themselves as well as others. Thus, dangerous behavior results from attempts to regain control in the present as well as, unconsciously, over the past.

People in trouble have limited repertoires. Their actions are heavily influenced by past experiences and are not responsive to present circumstances. They are bound by their histories. It is as if, when faced with an unopened bottle, the person reaches for a hammer because he has *always* reached for a hammer in the past. Such a move has a certain internal but idiosyncratic and self-destructive logic. The bottle will be opened but the contents will be useless.

Once maladaptive responses to stress occur, "explanations" are relatively easy, if somewhat illusory. But even though questions of precise etiology are difficult, treatment is not doomed. Physical illnesses are successfully dealt with despite the fact that most causes are not fully understood. Finding out precisely why someone beats his child or spouse, commits suicide, drinks himself to death, seduces his daughter, or does anything else is less important than the *early identification of such people at risk.* Interventions can then be instituted so that other, less maladaptive behaviors can be substituted. People have a tremendous capacity for recovery just as they have for destruction.

## APPROACHES TO PEOPLE
## IN DANGER

> I tell my residents never to get involved in how the patient got injured or hurt. I tell them "what you don't know can't hurt you."
>
> *A medical school professor*

An underlying assumption, when someone is potentially in trouble, is that something can or should be done. The former is a matter of technique, diagnosis, and treatment; the latter is a social and moral question.

The limit of responsibility is certainly an important issue. However, this question is usually raised when dealing with someone who is not liked or when the situation seems hopeless or overwhelming. Questions of responsibility are often designed to relieve the observer from the anxiety inherent in finding out that someone else is in trouble.

Antipathy and anxiety breed creative rationalizations that avoid the true issues: that the observer is disgusted, frightened, angered, feels helpless, and *does not know* what to do. For example, "Don't people have a right to die?" is a question asked by clinicians when they are dealing with patients who seem hopeless, overwhelming, or just not appealing. Although certain people are required by law to report the presence of child abuse and incest, the wish to deny their existence is much more powerful than the wish to intervene.

Another source of discomfort is caused by the observer's unconscious identification with people in trouble. People imagine themselves in the place of the victim or perpetrator. If this is too stimulating, empathy is walled off in order to avoid being flooded with anxiety. Becoming the other person, if only for an instant and unconsciously, is then wiped away

46

by denial and lack of understanding. "I can't believe" or "I can't understand" why something is happening is a clue that empathic resonance is too frightening.

Fantasies about incest-violence-suicide are frequently part of normal mental life. But if the observer is unsure about the potential boundaries of his own activities, he will be more critical, punitive, and unrealistic about those who have crossed those lines. Empathy is lost because people *do not want* to put themselves in the shoes of others. And with the loss of empathy goes the critical ingredient of any useful intervention. Without empathy and common sense, any intervention runs the risk of being punitive and destructive; the observer then becomes part of the problem, not the solution. Common sense diminishes because friends, family, and physicians have their own "emergency, maladaptive reactions" when faced with upsetting behaviors; the helpers themselves deal inadequately with stress. Small wonder then that physicians, family, and friends overlook, distort, and deny significant clues, or that— when action is taken—things often go awry.

Each situation is different and each problem raises distinct therapeutic issues. Consequently, interventions, to be effective, will have to be conceived of individually. In a sense, it is easier to discuss what *not to do* rather than to give blueprints for action. Destructive interventions are by their very nature similar and occur all too frequently in all these danger syndromes. By attending to what not to do, helpful interventions become more obvious.

## Commonly Made Errors

Wishes to deny, procrastinate, delay, and punish underlie the errors that are frequently made when dealing with dangerous behaviors. The following are some commonly employed unhelpful approaches to people in trouble along with what will happen if they are put into action and why. This hypothetical action-response format gives the reader a chance to "interact" with people in trouble.

*Action:* Ignore the presence of danger in the hope that it will go away.

*Result:* The failure to pick up overt and covert clues is the main reason why dangerous behaviors go untreated for so long. Participants find it difficult to seek help directly. If they do, they may ask for help in covert ways. "I haven't been feeling well recently" or "My husband and I have been arguing" might be met with empty reassurances and a pat on the back. No further exploration is attempted, although an opening has been provided.

Even if further information is obtained, observers usually ask, "What was the argument about?" not "What happened?" The latter line of questioning will lead to specifics about the presence of violence, drugs, alcohol; the former forecloses these possibilities. The inhibition is the observer's. When troubled situations finally come to light, usually through some disaster, the history is usually scattered with ignored clues and missed pleas for help.

*Action:* Recognize a dangerous situation but do nothing.

*Result:* Maladaptive behaviors are tenacious and will continue. They are rarely transient and the chance of recurrence is very high. Since these behaviors are often poor solutions to underlying problems and are symptomatic of destructive responses to stress, the associated difficulties *must* be dealt with in order to decrease the likelihood of recurrence or progression to a lethal outcome. Like a fever that indicates an underlying problem and that causes morbidity (and death) if left to run its course, these behaviors indicate malfunction elsewhere in the person's life. Believing that incest, abuse, or other problems are a one-time thing is wishful thinking.

*Action:* Accept outrageous explanations given by those suspected to be in trouble.

*Result:* People in trouble will feel even more isolated and misunderstood and the danger increases. The wish is strong to believe that an alcoholic has the "flu"; that the victim of spouse or child abuse has had an "accident." People are relieved to hear these excuses *even though at some level they do not believe them;* they wish them to be true so no further action will be necessary. The fabrication and consequent acceptance of excuses creates distance between those in trouble and their potential allies, since people become ashamed of the lies they tell, are giving covert clues, and then are angered by the ready acceptance of these lies by others.

*Action:* Attempt singlehandedly to "save" people in trouble.

*Result:* "Rescue" fantasies are commonly found in friends, family, *and* clinicians. However, the rescuers inevitably fall (or are pushed) off their white horses. The wish to make someone better, to take over, to become the deus ex machina is always doomed to failure. People in trouble must participate in their own treatment; they cannot be dragged into health. This wish to rescue indicates that the true nature of the problems is not fully appreciated; the problems are being minimized, since it is thought that they are so easily taken care of. The observer becomes frustrated and then angry at failing in his task. People in trouble feel as if they let the observer down by not getting better. Everyone feels defeated.

*Action:* Tell the person in trouble that "everyone knows what is going on," that "it must stop immediately."

*Result:* This intervention is felt as a criticism (it is) and only helps the observer's need to do something even if it is of no use. The observer's willingness to feel that this is an effective intervention is yet another covert form of denial of the situation; the behaviors are too complex to "stop" on comand and will likely continue. Although relieved to have been found out, people involved in these destructive behaviors feel extremely vulnerable to criticism and threats. They have fragile notions of self-worth, which, in fact, is one reason they are involved in these behaviors in the first place. Most people who participate in maladaptive behaviors want to stop; they have a sense that something is wrong. However, they are also at a loss as to what to do. Telling them to stop without offering alternatives is presenting them with a task at which they will fail. This increases their frustration, further decreases their self-esteem, and makes the situation more dangerous. However, telling people that treatment is possible will allow some to regain hope.

*Action:* Reason with the participants in dangerous behavior. Tell them that they are overlooking the consequences of their actions; what they are doing makes no sense.

*Result:* Although unreasonable, these behaviors make psychological sense. Suicide is sensible to someone who is desperate and feels hopeless. Child abuse, spousal violence, and incest are understandable once the victims' and perpetrators' histories are known. People drink in spite of, and to blot out, reason. Reasoning, in short, is poor leverage in changing people's behavior. Telling people what they already know about the consequences of their actions makes them feel even more helpless and ashamed.

*Action:* Gossip with friends and family about what you think is going on.

*Result:* People involved in maladaptive behaviors often are convinced that no one will help them. Judging by their childhood experiences, no one did. Further, they feel guilty, ashamed, and narcissistically vulnerable. When they discover they are being ridiculed, they feel that the humiliation is deserved, that they *are* bad and are beyond help. This will only drive them to withdraw and further solidify their maladaptive responses. Such gossip confirms their view of the world.

## Helpful Interventions

The psychological and physical morbidity and mortality experienced by people in trouble will depend in large part on what family, friends, and clinicians do, how they react and what attitudes they convey. Punitive, angry, and critical responses are normal but must be controlled. If people are ostracized, made to feel even more guilty and ashamed, they certainly will do poorly. Since all of these people suffer from interruptions and distortions in their ordinary relationships, anything that makes these connections even more tenuous makes matters worse. The realistic recognition of danger and empathic availability of others are the key ingredients to any successful approach.

Strategies and interventions for specific behaviors will be described in each chapter. Dealing with suicidal patients is different from treating alcoholics or victims of abuse or incest. However, there are general principles applicable to all situations where people are in potential trouble.

The observer who is too outraged or disgusted should first talk things over with someone else in order to cool off—otherwise, insults or arguments will replace helpful dialogue, and will simply reinforce the subjects' poor view of themselves. There are some general screening questions that may be helpful in uncovering dangerous behaviors. Ask: "Are there things going on at home or with you that you are worried about or that are making you unhappy?" Or, if the evidence of trouble is strong: "I am concerned about how things are going for you. You may think that you and your situation are beyond help, but help is always possible." These and similar questions will give those involved in dangerous behaviors an opportunity to air their difficulties; they also provide some hope.

The major impulse—to do nothing and let things slide—is destructive. The time of highest danger for maladaptive behaviors is relatively short, and all are episodic. The primary goal of any intervention is to reduce the immediate danger of suicide, abuse, and so forth. Doing something, no matter what, is usually better than not. Inaction can be fatal.

The first is the most critical step: the recognition of trouble. This should be followed by seeking competent help and advice. Physicians, mental health professionals, or clergy should be consulted. Unfortunately, since many of these people may not be well trained in dealing with such behaviors, *second or third*

51

*opinions are sometimes necessary if what is offered does not seem correct or sufficient.*

If child abuse or incest is suspected, child welfare agencies must be contacted. If danger of any sort is thought to be imminent, the police should be called immediately. *A false alarm is better than no alarm at all.* And when calling an agency or the police, make a record of who is spoken to and what is to be done. Do not hesitate to check back about what action has been taken. Procrastination and delay happen among professionals, also.

Personal availability to those in trouble can help to relieve some of the stresses that have led to the maladaptive behavior in the first place and can provide temporary "breathing space." For example, help with day care or providing a sanctuary may decrease the danger of an immediate lethal outcome. Since most people involved in these problems feel that they are beyond help and that nothing can be done, follow-through should also be checked. If appointments with mental health professionals are made, then it is helpful to find out whether they have been kept.

Common sense should prevail. If a person is dangerous to self or others he or she must be hospitalized immediately or in other ways protected. Force is sometimes necessary. Legal or convoluted moral arguments about civil liberties in the face of dangerous emergencies tend to obscure, rather than illuminate, the true issues. Fears of betraying trust or of legal retribution needlessly distract people from what should be done. "Pseudohelplessness" in the helper perpetuates dangerous behavior.

## Problems in Medical and Psychiatric Care

If the blind lead the blind, both
shall fall into the ditch.

*Matthew 15:14*

Physicians have an opportunity for the early identification and treatment of victims and perpetrators of abuse, incest, alcoholism, and suicide. However, this opportunity is often missed for a number of reasons: Doctors tend to be poorly trained in the areas of dangerous behaviors, do not know what to look for and what to do if problems are found. Time pressures certainly contribute to this problem. Doctors are unlikely to want to get into extended conversations when their waiting rooms are full. Also, physicians are not immune to the disgust, anger and anxiety that these problems evoke. In fact, this antipathy may be stronger in health professionals than in others, since the former feel obligated to *do* something and to take responsibility for illness. Thus, some doctors rationalize that certain problems are not medical matters and, therefore, should be left untouched. Furthermore, doctors underestimate what patients, especially if they are asked tactfully and compassionately, will tell them. But since physicians also are upset about what they may find, they do not look.

Some mental health professionals are not well equipped, either by training or temperament, to deal with these difficult situations. Emergencies create anxieties that make thinking difficult for both the patient and the professional. Many psychiatric training programs do not educate their residents adequately in emergency psychiatry. Psychologists and social workers have usually had even less exposure and training in these areas. In any case, *the ability to tolerate stress and to avoid maladaptive "therapeutic" responses is crucial in therapists.*

A problem among some mental health professionals is their denial of the intense affects or lethality involved in maladaptive situations. This denial may mean a failure to find out the specifics of what is going on; who is doing *what* to whom, *how* it is being done, and *when.* Usually the focus is exclusively on *why;* a convenient and intellectualized way to avoid *what* is really happening. Particularly in the case of incest, a patient's account may be perceived as generated by wishes and fantasy rather than by reality.

Other therapists do not have the clinical experience necessary to identify and then deal with these maladaptive behaviors. Alcoholism is a problem usually overlooked by medical and mental health personnel. Some psychotherapists know

53

little about child abuse and neglect and feel overwhelmed when dealing with these or with spousal violence or incest. Other mental health professionals have misperceived and misunderstood analytic theory and used this to adopt a passive stance toward their patients. Still other therapists are not accustomed to taking action, an obviously lethal inhibition in emergency situations. *Active* listening and delay can be useful but passivity may be fatal.

A gross instance of a therapist's denial is seen in the following example:

A psychiatrist was videotaping a session with a young patient who was describing in intimate and heart-rending detail abuse and neglect at the hands of her mother. In the midst of this depressing story the psychiatrist was paged on her beeper. She got up and said, "Keep talking when I leave. I'll listen to the tape later."

Most cases are not this obvious and destructive, but difficulties in dealing with such patients do arise because of some therapists' personal fears of the material. Their maneuvers may be unconsciously designed to protect themselves. Health professionals, therefore, need training in treating these difficult problems, and even experienced clinicians will find it helpful to obtain occasional consultation. Every clinician, no matter what his or her skill, loses perspective at times, and this is a particularly common occurrence with dangerous behaviors. Finally, there are many clinicians who are exceedingly skilled in dealing with the identification and treatment of these problems. Much of their work influenced the content of the following chapters.

Ultimately, the work of recovery is up to those involved in destructive behavior. Friends, family, and clinicians can provide support, hope, and understanding and must be ready to intervene when lethality is high, but people heal themselves. Maladaptive responses to stress have to be rejected in favor of healthier alternatives, old patterns altered enough to accommodate new behaviors.

# 2

# Alcoholism

## A CATALYST FOR
## DANGEROUS BEHAVIOR

Drunkenness doesn't create vices,
but it brings them to the fore.

*Seneca*

The illness called alcoholism is defined by the problems
alcohol creates. This chapter is about how alcohol acts as a
catalyst for maladaptive behaviors.

Not everyone who drinks excessively is involved with other
dangerous activities. However, not only the skid-row bum is
in trouble; people who do not seem to be problem drinkers
can also be at risk. Their drinking is not so obvious but is
nonetheless ruinous to themselves and their families. Alcoholics experience a progressive and insidious loss of control
over their drinking and behavior, as well as a decline in general functioning that is usually denied by family and friends.
This distortion of reality becomes apparent when the complications of alcoholism become so obvious that problems no
longer can be overlooked. People lose their jobs, their health,
and their lives. True physical addiction, on the other hand, is
not necessary in order to diagnose the disease. The following
cases illustrate the disruptions associated with alcohol; only in
the second instance was the alcoholic physically addicted:

A thirty-two-year-old unmarried kindergarten teacher turned her car over and landed upside-down in a creek. She escaped with a fractured hip and mild concussion. She was "high" on Valium and alcohol when she had the accident, which followed a fight with her boyfriend. She had blacked out at the wheel and narrowly missed hitting a pedestrian.

A forty-five-year-old divorced radiologist began having difficulties keeping up with his work. Following some weekends he came to the hospital late, smelling of alcohol; at times he disappeared for days. His colleagues ceased referring complicated cases to him although he continued to perform routine radiological procedures. Two nights after being hospitalized for abdominal pain, he began sweating profusely and became agitated, shouting for the police. He had to be forcibly restrained and medicated. After he recovered from the DT's, he refused further care. He committed suicide on his forty-seventh birthday.


The statistics are astounding. Twenty-five percent of people who commit suicide have significant problems with alcohol. In fact, alcohol abusers experience a sixty times greater suicide rate than the general public. Half of all traffic fatalities (and many accidents of all types) involve alcohol. A third of pedestrians who are killed "accidentally" are intoxicated. Mortality due to infant neglect is much higher in alcoholic families. Sixty percent of cases of child abuse, sixty-five percent of murder, about fifty percent of cases of rape, incest, and spousal violence involve alcohol.

One hundred million Americans use the drug. Ten million, in all social groups, abuse it significantly. Over *forty million* family members are affected by alcohol abuse; almost one-fifth of the country. Yet just five percent of abusers fall into the skid-row stereotype who fit the popular notion of "The Alcoholic." The others are less visible. They are higher functioning people who nonetheless have significant psychological, social, and medical problems due to alcohol abuse. More men than women have problems with alcohol, but the numbers are equalizing. Women's difficulties are harder to identify; their alcohol abuse has been more easily hidden in the home. The following case illustrates this and the nature of what ultimately turned out to be a fatal disease:

By the time Edith was eleven, she had grown used to the household smells that followed her mother's weekend drinking bouts. She was relieved on a particular Sunday morning that she didn't have to call anyone for help. Her mother was sound asleep in her bedroom. She knew she would not see her mother much that day. She planned on doing things alone anyway. Edith was self-sufficient, having learned early in life to take care of herself—particularly when her mother was drinking heavily, which recently was most of the time. Her mother and father were separated.

Edith's younger brother was still asleep. As she walked out on the landing, she noticed that some lights were still on downstairs—when she went to investigate, she saw that the back door was open, her cat already outside. She methodically began to clean the kitchen, straightening up, throwing out bottles. She thought about inviting someone over to play with her but did not want to be embarrassed if her mother woke up before she was completely sober. She didn't know how to deal with her mother when she was drunk.

Edith's mother had just returned after two months in a Connecticut hospital where she had gone for a "rest" following the separation. She left before she had completed the program. She was irritable and depressed when she came to pick up Edith at her father's apartment two days after having returned from Connecticut. Yesterday, while Edith and her brother waited in the car to go shopping, her mother ran back into the house

57

because she had "forgotten" something. Edith knew she had gone back for a drink.

Her mother looked puffy and pale after the hospital—very much as she did when she went away. She was tense, preoccupied; not very attentive. There had been more talk about a divorce.

The mother had had difficulty caring for the children since an automobile accident six years before in which she severely hurt her back. She had begun taking pain and sleeping medication to control her discomfort, often going from one doctor to the next. Edith would sometimes go to the pharmacy to collect the medicine after the doctors telephoned in the prescriptions.

Once her mother took too many pills and had to be rushed to the hospital. Edith overheard the doctor say that her mother was "drunk" and that she had taken the sleeping pills "accidentally." Yesterday, she had picked up another prescription for her mother.

Today, when her mother didn't get up, Edith went into the bedroom where she found her dead of an overdose. The coroner said it was an "accidental" death due to alcohol and sleeping pills.

Many deaths that result from the combination of alcohol and drugs are erroneously labelled "accidental." Much has been made of "automatic" drug-taking behavior, cases in which people become confused and inadvertently take an overdose. Such cases probably exist. However, this explanation usually conceals a bona fide suicide attempt. After an overdose, this reasoning should only be accepted following a long and careful psychological examination. Edith's mother was suicidal, a fact overlooked by her family and her physicians. "Accidental" overdoses, no matter what the circumstances, are extremely rare.

People such as Edith's mother who abuse alcohol often take other drugs, usually the sedative-hypnotics: sleeping pills and tranquilizers. These drugs, including alcohol, act in pharmacologically similar ways and can be extremely toxic if mixed. Other drugs are also frequently abused. Marijuana and alcohol are often used together. Amphetamines may be taken to counter the depressant effects of alcohol and sedative hypnotics, or for the euphoric and energizing effects of that class of drug. The same with cocaine. Drugs like Miltown, Valium, Quaaludes, and barbiturates (Seconal, Tuinal, and so forth) are also agents of abuse.

As was just illustrated, patients frequently get their medicines from physicians, often by "doctor shopping." Practitioners who do not fully evaluate their patients will miss the existence of self-destructive behavior. Over 80 percent of people who overdose successfully do so with *one* prescription recently obtained from a physician. The doctor makes a double mistake: He misses the covert presentation of suicide and, in addition, provides the means for death.

Alcohol clearly has a profound effect on the presence of dangerous behavior. Why this is so varies on a case-by-case basis. What is clear, however, is that if alcohol and other drug abuse is recognized and treated, the likelihood of dangerous behavior diminishes.

## THE CAUSES OF ALCOHOL ABUSE

Alcoholism is not a single disease. The drug alcohol is abused in different situations in various ways for many reasons. However, the detrimental social and psychological effects of alcohol are so similar that these effects form the core definition of the illness. The reasons for drinking are then submerged by the adverse effects of the drug, and it becomes difficult to distinguish between the causes and the results of alcoholism.

One has to look for multiple etiologies to determine why people drink. Many experiment with drugs and some use them regularly—only a small percentage abuse them and fewer become physically addicted. Why this variability exists is not readily explained.

Alcohol use usually begins in socially accepted ways. Peer pressure plays a role here. Drinking may then be increased at times of turmoil and stress in an attempt to cope with external difficulties or soothe internal emotions. Many abuse this drug because they are unable to tolerate strong feelings and fear being overwhelmed by them; their threshold for frustration is low. They use drugs to modulate affects. Affect intolerance is also present in those with a history of early parental abuse and neglect. Interestingly, early deprivation has also been suggested as one of the causes of alcohol abuse. Many alcoholics seemingly have unmet dependency needs. Besides the "releasing" effects of alcohol, the problem of frustration tolerance may account for the high association of alcoholism with dangerous behavior, since poor frustration tolerance is also found in people who are prone to maladaptive responses.

Alcohol is used by many in a misguided attempt at self-medication; people treat themselves. Alcohol has a calming effect on anger, anxiety, and depression. This relief drinking seems to palliate feelings of low self-esteem, depression, loneliness, and emptiness. About a third of alcohol abusers suffer from a major emotional illness in addition to alcoholism. Schizophrenia and affective disorders (depression, manic-depressive disease) are not infrequently uncovered when alcohol abuse ceases. Other drinkers suffer from severe character disorders, borderline schizophrenia, antisocial personalities, and other difficulties. The consequences of alcohol abuse thus complicate the diagnosis and prognosis of the primary, underlying disorder. This may partially explain the extremely high suicide rate among alcoholics suffering from psychiatric illnesses, since these, too, have high rates of suicide. In addition, alcohol chemically exacerbates depressive tendencies. This association with psychiatric disease may also account for the lack of improvement among some alcoholic patients under treatment. When the underlying psychiatric illness is ignored, the patient will continue the attempts at self-medication.

Alcoholism runs in families. Some experts distinguish primary alcoholism, which is viewed as a genetic disease with an early onset and virulent course, from problem drinking, which presumably does not share these characteristics. There is increasing evidence for a strong genetic influence, which points to possible underlying biochemical differences in the way alcohol is metabolized in those who are constitutionally vulnerable to abuse. Children of alcoholics often become alcoholics or teetotalers. Identical twins have a higher concordance rate for alcoholism than do fraternal twins. Identical twins might be raised differently from fraternal twins, and consequently their life experiences can account for their higher concordance rate. However, genetic endowment does have a critical influence; children of alcoholics suffer from a higher rate of alcoholism even when adopted at a very early age, as compared to adopted children of nonalcoholic parents.

Finally, alcoholism, depression, and other dangerous behaviors cluster in the same families. The following family tree illustrates some of these associations:

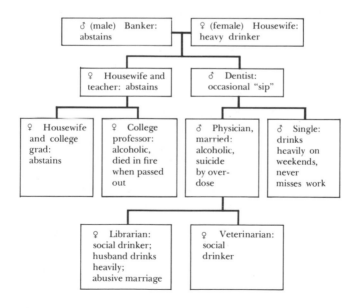

## THE ACTIONS OF ALCOHOL

Drink, sir, is a great provoker of three things
... Marry, sir, nude painting, sleep, and
urine. Lechery, sir, it provokes and unpro-
vokes: it provokes the desire, but it takes away
the performance.

*Shakespeare: Macbeth II, iii*

If the causes of alcoholism are obscure, the effects of alcohol are not. In excess, alcohol adversely affects all spheres of
functioning. Chronic or excessive use leads to impaired functioning (abuse), increasing tolerance to the drug, and withdrawal symptoms (physical dependence). Alcohol causes
people to withdraw, feel anxious and depressed. People drink
to relieve these dysphoric states, but it appears that alcohol,
as a drug, is a depressant, and that it is also likely to induce
depression. For example:

A sixty-three-year-old nurse was admitted to a hospital, intoxicated and highly suicidal. The attending physician noted that the patient was depressed "only when
inebriated." When sober the patient was discharged. She
hung herself the next day.

The missed clinical fact was that since the patient drank
most of the time she was usually depressed and always potentially suicidal. It is not always easy to distinguish between the
pharmacological actions of alcohol and the underlying psychological disturbance.

Excessive and chronic intake of alcohol results in the development of physical tolerance to the intoxicating properties of
the drug. Greater amounts of alcohol are required to achieve
the same mental and physical effects. It therefore takes a
higher blood alcohol concentration to intoxicate a physically
tolerant individual who metabolizes alcohol more efficiently.
But this enhanced capacity for alcohol is finite and a limit is

finally reached. Alcoholics may "hold" their liquor better but also can die of alcohol overdoses. In fact, severe inebriation may be the result of a purposeful suicide attempt that is overlooked since the person is viewed as "only drunk."

Under normal conditions, people metabolize and detoxify about one ounce of whiskey per hour—some a little more, others a little less. From the stomach and small intestine, alcohol is absorbed rapidly into the blood stream. The degree of intoxication depends on the rate of absorption in addition to the absolute amount of alcohol consumed. Anything that increases the rate of absorption causes greater intoxication. Thus, water or carbonation, each of which enhances absorption, makes people drunker, faster. This accounts for the kick in highballs and champagne. Conversely, food slows the rate and makes alcohol more mangeable and less inebriating.

Alcohol causes dehydration and hypothermia, two obviously dangerous effects for those who spend any time out of doors. Alcohol is a diuretic, causing increased urine output, as any drinker knows. It also dilates blood vessels in the skin, thereby creating the sense of warmth associated with alcohol. This is a potentially lethal illusion. The body *loses* heat in an accelerated fashion as blood is drawn away from vital organs to the skin, where heat is then needlessly dissipated. For example, drinking on cross-country ski trips, although enjoyable, increases the dangers of exposure and hypothermia if the party should get into unexpected trouble and be delayed in the wilderness.

More than any other organ system, the brain is exquisitely sensitive to alcohol. One reason for this is the brain's highly developed blood supply, which rapidly transports alcohol to its tissues. Like other general anesthetics, alcohol is a central nervous system depressant—not stimulant, as is commonly thought. Alcohol initially affects the inhibitory and integrating areas of the brain so that other parts are "released" from this higher control. Inhibiting the inhibitions results in erroneously ascribing stimulant properties to alcohol; alcohol depresses higher functions, thereby releasing lower ones.

## ALCOHOL AND DANGEROUS
## BEHAVIOR

The releasing effects of alcohol make destructive activity possible. Alcohol "heats up" situations and loosens behaviors. Perpetrators and victims who are prone to be provocative will be more so. People are more likely to act when drunk. Altered feelings, thinking, and behavior reflect alcohol's disorganizing and releasing effects on the brain. Alcohol affects cognitive abilities, alertness, level of consciousness, and motor coordination and causes the brain to work in desynchronized ways. Judgment is diminished, as is the ability to learn from previous experiences and to anticipate the consequences of future actions. Insight, memory, and the ability to concentrate are dimmed and then lost. One's mood becomes labile and emotional outbursts occur. Higher doses of alcohol produce coma, respiratory depression, and death.

Alcohol also alters the ability to tolerate pain and reduces performance anxiety, two properties that can increase the danger of destructive behavior if the drinker is so inclined. The ability to tolerate pain is increased for two reasons: The pain threshold is raised, and subjective concern about painful experiences is lowered. Therefore, things may be attempted with the ingestion of moderate amounts of alcohol that wouldn't be tried without it. Activities, destructive or not, are carried out with a decreased fear of failure and fewer worries about the consequence of success. Alcohol can be resorted to during the build-up phase of any crisis situation in order to relieve tension and anxiety. However, by weakening controls, alcohol increases the likelihood that maladaptive behaviors will occur. And once trouble occurs, alcohol may be resorted to in order to soothe the emotional aftermath of the crisis; if used excessively, more problems are potentially created. Both the soothing and releasing effects of alcohol are illustrated by a fourteen-year-old daughter of a police lieutenant:

64

The girl was sexually molested by her father over a five-year period. They even had intercourse while her mother was at home. The girl's anxiety was so great that she began to take her father's pain pills on a daily basis. Soon, she began sharing his bourbon, which he encouraged, noting that it made his daughter a more relaxed and willing partner.

Aggressive behavior increases with alcohol, and drink can be used to rationalize and excuse such activity. "He only beats me when he is drunk" is both true and an excuse. Sexual activity is also enhanced by alcohol. However, too much alcohol inhibits performance, thereby lowering self-esteem and increasing the danger of violence between partners. Spouse abuse tends to be particularly violent and cruel when alcohol is involved.

When someone is drunk and a weapon is present, the danger of homicide increases dramatically. A particular form of family violence associated with alcohol, the "Saturday-night Syndrome," involves mutual provocation and abuse between husband and wife. Both are drunk and both are extremely aggressive.

Alcohol is a definite factor in child abuse and neglect. Intoxicated parents obviously make poor caretakers. At best, family turmoil and preoccupation with the effect of alcohol detract from parental ability to provide an adequate home environment for a child. At worst, alcoholism is fatal. In addition, many children of alcoholics have to function prematurely on their own because they, in turn, must care for their parents. Edith in the case mentioned earlier was forced to function this way. This role-reversal creates a brittle pseudo-independence in children, which hides emotional needs that have not been met effectively. Matters are made worse if both parents are alcohol abusers or if these are single-parent families.

Alcohol also lubricates inappropriate familial sexual behav-

65

ior. Fathers may blame alcohol, or anything else, in order to "explain" incest. One father said, "I got into the wrong bed when I was loaded—I didn't know what I had done until morning." He said that he had intercourse with his thirteen-year-old daughter "only" when he was drunk.

Intoxication and withdrawal states are also associated with dangerous behavior. After ingesting very small amounts of alcohol some people literally go crazy. This syndrome, pathological intoxication, luckily is rarely found. People become confused, delirious, aggressive, and assaultive. Their destruction can be mindless. They are amnestic during the episode, which may last a few moments to a day or more and is usually terminated by a long sleep. The sudden onset, amnesia, and termination by sleep are also characteristic of seizure disorders. In fact, pathological intoxication may represent a form of psychomotor epilepsy that is precipitated by alcohol.

Pathological intoxication is one of the many physical disorders that can precipitate the Dyscontrol Syndrome, a controversial neurological entity that some say is one of the causes of spousal violence, child abuse, homicide, unprovoked assault, dangerous driving, sexual assault, and destruction of property. Although the Dyscontrol Syndrome exists, it should not be overdiagnosed. Most people know what they are doing when they are drunk. It is they, not the bottle, talking.

Danger exists in another aspect of alcohol abuse. In the midst of withdrawal states people are delirious, confused, agitated, paranoid, and frequently violent. The danger of impulsive homicidal and suicidal behavior is high, especially since the violence occurs suddenly. These syndromes may develop with little warning, particularly if alcoholism is not suspected. Withdrawal can occur when a problem drinker abstains or simply *lowers* alcohol intake. For example, during hospitalizations for other problems, many previously undiagnosed alcoholics become delirious, agitated, and confused. Like the radiologist, they hallucinate or become paranoid. Others just develop the "shakes," a milder form of withdrawal. The confusion and paranoia of withdrawal states make violence a definite danger. Fortunately, many of these patients are too confused to act; others do commit suicide during these dreamlike states.

## THE FAMILY

Alcoholism has profoundly negative effects on family and friends. Family members feel ashamed and stigmatized by it; at times, they may irrationally feel responsible for the alcohol abuse itself. In addition to the abuser, about 25 percent of other family members will also have problems with alcohol. Often "milder" forms of alcohol abuse may be overlooked when one family member is labeled as the one "really in trouble." The fact that alcoholism and depression are linked also makes it likely that these families will be burdened by depression.

General family functioning is always impaired by the presence of an alcoholic. Such families are likely to function under the constant threat of destabilization. Frequent moves are common. The abuser may lose jobs, have legal difficulties, or develop life-threatening medical complications secondary to the alcohol. Separation and divorce are frequent as are repeated hospitalizations and early death.

Relatives usually feel unjustly responsible for the alcohol abuse and are hopeful that it will stop. If the drinking is episodic, family members fear the next bout which no doubt will arrive. When there is no improvement, resentment and rage replace hope, and there is further guilt as the family and abuser become demoralized, isolated and estranged. Most of this takes place in secret, which makes it even more difficult for the family to obtain help for themselves or for the drinker. Only when there is a severe crisis is the cover blown and the chance for obtaining help improved.

67

## COMMON REACTIONS
## TO ALCOHOL ABUSE

Alcohol has always had an ambivalent place in our society. It has been called the elixir of life and the root of all evil. It enjoys the position of being the number one recreational drug in America. People use it to unwind, relax, and break the ice. But when drug-taking behavior gets out of control, moralistic condemnation takes the place of social approval. Alcohol abusers are maligned, slandered, and blamed for their difficulties. They are accused of "voluntarily" creating their own illnesses. Alcoholism is not seen as a disease but rather as a *moral failing*. Consequently, alcohol abuse is the most overlooked and undertreated *curable* disease in the United States today.

Other emotional reactions to the problem drinker depend on the specific behavior of the drinker when intoxicated. Some people become belligerent, others tranquilized. And at times, the drug-free personality is so obnoxious that family and friends are relieved when sobriety disappears; the calming effects of alcohol make it easier to live with certain people.

The following are some of the more common responses to alcohol abusers, with an explanation of why they occur:

1. *Minimize alcoholism,* since the person doesn't "look like" an alcoholic. This response allows the observer to overlook the vast majority of problem drinkers and thus avoid the anxiety of discovery. Only 5 percent of alcohol abusers look like "alcoholics." The stereotype of the alcoholic excludes the housewife who is always sipping a glass of wine or the businessman who drinks heavily both at lunch and dinner. Minimizing problems in others may also be a way of denying such problems in oneself.

2. *Condemn the alcoholic as dissolute, depraved, and a profligate.* Because the illness appears to be voluntary, people feel justified in this critical response. Observers are often horrified by

the lack of control exhibited by alcoholics—they are too infantile, sexual, or aggressive—and feel guilty about such impulses themselves. They may be unconsciously condemning their own covert wishes.

Such condemnation was reflected in law until fairly recently; for years public intoxication was a crime. Only recently has alcoholism been decriminalized and labeled as a problem in need of medical attention. However, alcohol abuse still has not been accepted fully as a legitimate medical illness or as a symptom of an underlying psychiatric disorder. With certain other illnesses (tuberculosis, venereal disease, epilepsy) it still shares the characteristics of a moral failing. To be sick is to have a weak character.

3. *Express fury* at the abuser because of the stigma and shame of alcoholism and the fact that the abuser is so self-destructive and egocentric. Anger may become so intense that family and friends may consciously and unconsciously wish the alcoholic were dead. If an alcoholic does die, such ambivalence creates special difficulties in the grief response; the observer feels both glad and sad about the death. If the circumstances of death are violent or sudden (suicide, accident), survivors will have even more problems grieving the loss.

4. *Feel demoralized and pessimistic* about what can be done. Therapeutic nihilism allows the observer to avoid assisting the alcoholic and thus assuages the guilt of not trying to help. "What's the use?" excuses inaction. However, though substance abuse is a chronic illness, it still has a better prognosis than many other diseases. With appropriate care, about two-thirds of alcoholics improve; only one-third do not respond to treatment at all. The clinical course of alcoholism is marked by exacerbations and remissions that, if anticipated, will not lead so readily to demoralization. Unfortunately, this less pessimistic outlook is not widely shared. The majority of public opinion still resides with the picture of the end-stage alcoholic whose prognosis is certainly poor indeed.

5. *Make excuses for the alcoholic's destructive behavior* on the grounds of intoxication. This pernicious reaction minimizes

both the problem with alcohol and the dangerousness of the behavior. The observer does not wish to acknowledge the gravity of the situation and colludes with the alcoholic in denying the existence of any "real" problems. "It is just the bottle talking" allows the observer to avoid being angry at the alcoholic and to overlook the presence of serious difficulties.

6. *Feel responsible* for the alcoholic's behavior. This is a common response among close family and friends. It is typical in any crisis, no matter what the circumstances, to wonder about one's responsibility for the current difficulties. Alcoholics will also blame anyone but themselves for "driving" them to drink, as though it were someone else's doing. Unfortunately, family and friends accept this responsibility, thus increasing resentment and anger on one side and decreasing the chances of recovery on the other.

## DANGER SIGNALS
## CLUES TO ALCOHOL ABUSE

People with drinking problems rarely complain of "alcoholism." Rather, they suffer from the adverse effects of drinking. Not all of these problems need be present. Often the best indicator of alcoholism is the observer's "gut" response to certain given situations. Further exploration, usually by a professional, will be necessary to make a final diagnosis. The following are some clues that point to the presence of alcohol abuse:

• The aggravation of *domestic problems,* leading to fights, separation, or divorce. Frequent family crises are clues to alcohol abuse.

• The presence of *suicidal behavior, child abuse,* or other dangerous behaviors.

• A *poor work history* with frequent job change. These people are fired (or quit before this happens) for taking too many sick days, coming late for work, or being generally irresponsible, disorganized, and unproductive. Being late on Mondays or after holidays is not uncommon. People may drink on the job.

• *Frequent accidents,* automobile or otherwise. Broken bones, "slips" on the ice, and "bumping" into doors should raise suspicions. Arrests for driving under the influence and the loss of drivers' licenses are, obviously, solid clues.

• A history of *fights, temper outbursts, impulsive behavior,* or trouble with the law.

• *Adolescent turmoil,* indicating the possibility of adolescent alcoholism. Truancy, delinquency, school difficulties, and suicidal behavior may coexist with drug abuse and also be clues to incest.

• *Binge drinking.* Getting looped on weekends or taking a drink in the morning may be viewed in a skewed sense as rugged, but this behavior probably exists so the drinker can find the courage to start the day or treat the jitters of withdrawal.

• *Blackouts.* These are relatively early signs of abuse. The mechanism of this drug-induced amnestic syndrome is not known, although there may be both physical and psychological determinants. Complex activities may be carried out with no subsequent recall. The blackout as an excuse for behavior that may be considered morally wrong has obvious psychological benefits. The seriousness of incest, spouse or child abuse, or other destructive behaviors may be minimized, since the perpetrator will have no memory of them.

• *Vague and chronic physical complaints,* usually associated with the gastrointestinal tract. These may have multiple etiologies and can be secondary to the anxiety and depression so frequently present in alcohol abusers. Even though alcoholics may seek medical attention for these problems, the diagnosis of alcoholism is usually not made during the early stages of the illness.

• *The presence of the physical consequences of alcohol abuse,* among them pancreatitis, cirrhosis of the liver, neuropathies (nerve problems), gastritis, ulcers, and cardiomyopathies (heart problems). These result not only from the toxic effects of alcohol but are generally caused by associated nutritional deficiencies as well.

• *Withdrawal phenomena*, from the shakes to full-blown delirium tremens (DT's), due to withdrawal from alcohol and other drugs. It is important to remember that delirium may be caused by intoxication as well as by a withdrawal state. In addition, many other causes of delirious states are easily missed if alcoholism is thought to be the only illness present. The presence of physical alcohol *addiction*, with its attendant alcohol tolerance and physiological dependence, is not a precondition to diagnose alcoholism.

## WHAT THEY SAY
## WHAT THEY MEAN

The verbalizations of alcoholics are usually designed to hide the extent of their difficulties. The following are some examples of what may be said by the problem drinker and what is really meant:

| *Says* | *Means* |
| --- | --- |
| I've got the flu. | I've been on a binge and am hung over. |
| I only drink now and then. | My drinking is out of control. |
| I drink only one or two martinis a day. | Each one consists of twelve ounces of gin. |
| Things are going pretty well. | I've just lost my job and feel very depressed. |
| Do you think I am stupid enough to drink and drive at the same time? | Yes. |
| Just give me one more drink and I'll stop for good. | I am a chronic alcoholic and can't abstain without help. |

72

## GENERAL APPROACHES
## TO THE ALCOHOLIC

To dispute with a drunkard is
to debate with an empty house.

*Publilius Syrus*

A key element in any successful approach to problem drinkers is paying attention to and respecting their need for denial. A frontal assault is rarely helpful. Substance abuse in general—and alcoholism in particular—is one of those areas where conflict between the abuser and family effectively stymies progress. Arguments will polarize and isolate, making everyone feel even more resentful and hopeless.

What is important, however, is to keep clear who is doing what and to whom. One person does not "drive" the other "to drink." This is a convenient excuse that etiologically does not make sense. However, what family and friends do can hinder or promote recovery of the drinker. People respond, in part, according to what is expected of them. "Forgiving" the alcoholic his excesses—being "nice" and "understanding"— undercuts recovery. The mistaken notion, promoted by all sides, that "healthy" family members somehow must get the alcoholic to stop drinking, is doomed to failure. This distorted sense of responsibility is one reason why these families become so demoralized.

The following are some of the more common *un*successful approaches to the alcoholic, with explanations of why these are unlikely to work. The next section contains suggestions about more useful and helpful maneuvers.

### Commonly Made Errors

*Action:* Do nothing and act as if everything were normal.

*Result:* People confuse being "nice" with what will be helpful. Problems should not be covered up and denied. This per-

73

petuates the unrealistic assumption that the alcoholic is not in trouble. The alcoholic will be able to fool himself, as long as others participate in the charade, and will continue to drink.

*Action:* Warn the alcoholic about what will happen if drinking continues.

*Result:* Alcohol abusers regularly distort and lie about the amount they consume, and they will continue to drink. They do this to hide the true nature of their problem from themselves and others. They are frightened that what seems to be a necessary and life-saving medication will be taken from them *with nothing offered in return.* Telling an alcoholic to stop drinking is like telling a drowning person not to hold on to a life preserver because it may spring a leak. By drinking, the alcoholic is self-medicating a condition and solving a problem that he feels can't be dealt with in any other way. The circumstances that stimulate the drinking have to be recognized and altered as part of any alcohol treatment program. Point out to the alcoholic that there are ways in which he can be helped and things need not continue as they are.

*Action:* Force the alcohol abuser to admit that he is an alcoholic.

*Result:* In order to be successfully rehabilitated, the alcoholic eventually will have to appraise his condition realistically. However, alcohol abusers, deeply ashamed and guilty about their behavior, have a great need to save face. A strong and premature confrontation will make the alcoholic feel rejected, angry, and humiliated, thus increasing his sense of isolation and estrangement. Drinking may increase and the alcoholic may feel even more guilty. Demanding a confession is usually more punitive than therapeutic. However, helping the alcoholic to recognize that there is a problem is a beginning step in breaking through denial.

*Action:* Tell the alcoholic that he is destroying his family and should quit drinking and go into the hospital.

*Result:* Many alcoholics feel helpless and hopeless and view their lives as totally out of control. They suffer from poor self-esteem, which makes them particularly sensitive to criticism. Blaming them for destroying their families confirms the poor self-image that alcoholics typically have. The likelihood of suicide as a solution to the dilemma increases. Confrontation, but not of an angry, punitive type, is a good tool. A useful approach is to point out to the alcoholic that he or she is frightened of being out of control and of hurting loved ones, and that control may be regained through such means as hospitalization.

*Action:* Attempt to "rescue" the drinker.

*Result:* Making drinking the problem of others relieves the abuser of responsibility for his or her behavior. Alcoholics, prone to deny and externalize, will gladly place the blame on anyone who will accept it. However, others will become angry and guilty about their failure to stop the drinking. In addition, the alcoholic will also feel worse because he has let his rescuer down. When people feel *less responsible,* and no longer compelled to save the alcoholic, their anger will decrease and the alcoholic and the family may then become more realistic about the nature of the difficulty.

## Helpful Interventions

Friends and family must come to terms with their own anger, shame, depression, and resentment before they can be helpful to the alcoholic. They have to decide what they will tolerate from the alcoholic and what is unacceptable behavior. Sometimes all that friends and family can do is to protect themselves. Psychotherapy, and self-help groups such as Alanon and Alateen, are useful *even if* the alcoholic continues to refuse care. Seeking such help indicates that the family's denial and possible collusion is coming to an end. Giving up feelings of responsibility for the alcoholic's behavior may allow the family to function more effectively. If the alcoholic's

75

"blackmail" is not dealt with, then the family will remain frozen in an attitude of sullen resentment and guilt. Sometimes such self-protective psychotherapeutic work may take place years after the alcoholic has left or died.

Unfortunately, some alcoholics have to hit rock bottom before they will seek help. Therefore, ignoring the true state of affairs, making excuses, or otherwise buffering the alcoholic supports the idea that the alcoholic cannot care for himself or herself and delays the severe crises that may provide the impetus for seeking help. Marital separation or divorce—not simply threats—may be necessary before the alcoholic seeks treatment. Threats followed by capitulation help no one. The same principles apply in a work situation. If the job is not performed adequately, the alcoholic can be offered help as a condition of continued employment. But if the work does not improve or remain adequate, the worker should be removed from employment rather than supported by excuses.

Children of alcoholics are sometimes placed in dangerous situations. As in Edith's family, the nonalcoholic parent may desert or divorce, leaving children with the alcoholic. Often the courts collude in this unhealthy situation, particularly when they give custody to alcoholic mothers without fully realizing what impact this will have on children's development. The courts, in these cases, are placing children in neglectful and sometimes abusive homes without the protection of the nonalcoholic parent. Children are then forced to care for their disabled parents.

Setting realistic goals for sobriety is important. Aiming for complete and life-long abstinence may be a noble goal, but doing so also places an unrealistic and heavy burden on the whole family. If it is accepted that alcoholism is a chronic disease, with exacerbations and remissions, setbacks won't cause the same degree of demoralization and despair. The goal of short-term abstinence is more realistic.

# MEDICAL INTERVENTIONS
# WITH THE ALCOHOLIC

*A joke heard at a dinner party:*
Patient (a derelict): Doc, can you spare a quarter?
Doctor: Sure, if you have change for a five.

The medical management of alcoholism founders on the dislike that alcoholics engender in physicians. Covert clues to alcoholism are often overlooked, or, when diagnosed, alcoholics receive notoriously poor care. About one-half of problem drinkers go undiagnosed by their physicians.

The reasons for this dislike are not hard to find. Alcoholics are thought to create their own illnesses and are not "really" sick. Furthermore, alcoholics are hard to "cure" and are difficult and demanding to treat. Such negative attitudes are changing but still characterize a predominant feeling of the medical community.

While this section is not designed to provide complete information on the medical care of alcoholism, it does contain guidelines that will educate family and friends and provide a framework for physicians.

There are some mistakes commonly made by medical practitioners. These *un*successful interventions are followed by more helpful approaches.

## Commonly Made Medical Errors

*Action:* Prescribe sleeping pills to an insomniac without undertaking an adequate psychosocial evaluation.

*Result:* The patient might make a suicide attempt. Unless a proper history is taken and efforts made to look for the danger signals of alcoholism, it can be overlooked. Alcoholics often come to their physicians with vague somatic complaints that are symptomatic of underlying depression, anxiety, and alcohol abuse. Patients are already self-medicating themselves for depression. Their complaint may be a plea for help.

77

*Action:* Neglect to obtain a drug and alcohol history for fear of offending a middle-class patient.

*Result:* The patient may have alcoholic withdrawal seizures the day after admission to the hospital. Hesitancy to inquire about drugs, alcohol, suicidal thinking, and other destructive behaviors can have tragic consequences. Patients sense what the doctor is (or is not) comfortable talking about and will rarely offer information unless the doctor indicates that he wants to listen. This has more to do with the doctor's level of comfort than with the patient's anxiety. Some doctors *do not want to know* what is wrong.

*Action:* Discuss treatment issues with an intoxicated patient who is then sent home.

*Result:* Chronic alcoholics, when intoxicated, may appear alert since they are physiologically used to high doses of alcohol. However, they are suffering from a toxic delirium (they are drunk) and should be treated as such. Memory and judgment are impaired. Discussions about treatment, detoxification, and rehabilitation should wait until sobriety is established. Furthermore, sending a patient home prematurely and drunk reflects a dislike of the patient and also places the doctor at risk if the patient has an automobile accident. The wish to "get rid" of the alcoholic must be guarded against so that the patient is properly evaluated and treated.

*Action:* Assume that the patient's confused and disoriented behavior is due to alcohol intoxication.

*Result:* Alcoholics, especially if they smell of alcohol, are assumed to be "only" drunk, and other potentially fatal illnesses are then overlooked. Subdural hematomas and fractured skulls, liver failure, and intercurrent infections such as pneumonia, tuberculosis, or urinary tract infections also contribute to delirious, confused states. Furthermore, alcoholics can withdraw from alcohol even while intoxicated. A relative drop in blood alcohol levels, rather than total absence of alcohol, precipitates withdrawal syndromes. Another frequent error is ignoring the possibility of coexistent intoxication or withdrawal from other medications, particularly barbiturates, other tranquilizers, or sedative-hypnotics that the patient may also be abusing.

## Helpful Medical Interventions

The medical management of the alcohol abuser is concerned with four major areas: 1) the management of the periods of acute intoxication; 2) the treatment of physical problems associated with chronic and heavy alcohol usage; 3) the management of alcohol withdrawal syndromes; and 4) the identification of the covert problem drinker. (This fourth task will be expanded on here.)

A thorough alcohol and drug history should be obtained from all patients, whether they appear to be alcoholic or not, preferably on the first visit. However, patients may be more forthright after a good doctor-patient relationship has been established, and the doctor should keep in mind that his or her initial impression may underestimate the presence of alcohol abuse.

The following questions can be used, in a nonthreatening way, to uncover difficulty with alcohol.

• Did anyone ever think that you drank too much?
• Did you ever drink more than you thought was good for you?
• Did you ever have regrets about anything you did while drinking?
• Did you ever have problems with alcohol in the past?
• Did you ever sneak a drink after trying to stop?
• Did you ever suffer from blackouts or the shakes or other withdrawal problems?

These are asked in addition to questions about drinking habits, amounts, and so forth. Physicians should avoid debate with patients about how much alcohol is consumed. The focus

79

ought to be on the functional problems the patient and family are experiencing, not on how much is drunk. Patients may fabricate; the physician should then look for the other clues to alcohol abuse.

Alcohol abusers need a complete physical evaluation, with particular attention to their nutritional status. They may require vitamin supplements to treat the Wernicke-Korsakoff Syndrome (dementia, ataxia, ophthalmoplegia, neuropathy) and hydration and tranquilization if they show such signs of alcohol withdrawal as tachycardia, tremulousness, and a fever. If patients develop withdrawal syndromes, an underlying infection or other illness that can precipitate withdrawal states should be looked for.

Antabuse may be prescribed to help maintain abstinence if there are no contraindications—such as severe heart or blood pressure problems—and if the doctor has experience using it. The patient will find it extremely uncomfortable to drink while taking this drug, although some patients are able to drink "under" the medication.

Patients may be referred to alcohol treatment programs such as Alcoholics Anonymous (A.A.), or to a psychiatrist if they wish. Patients may be told, "I am concerned about your body's reaction to alcohol. I think you need help with this." Patients may perceive such a referral as a rejection unless the referring physician also continues with the patient. Therefore, it is important that the patient be seen on a regular and frequent basis, particularly in the beginning of treatment. Referrals to alcohol treatment programs can also be enhanced if the doctor calls or writes follow-up letters to the patient. Family members should also be involved in treatment. This helps decrease the patient's and family's denial about the extent of the problems and creates pressure on the patient to continue the alcohol treatment.

Doctors should make it easy for patients to continue office visits even if the drinking continues. Comments such as "I won't see you if you drink again" are counterproductive.

# EMERGENCY PSYCHIATRIC
# INTERVENTIONS

The following are some frequent errors made during psychiatric evaluations. The next section contains an outline of more successful interventions.

## Commonly Made Psychiatric Errors

*Action:* Overlook the danger of violence when evaluating a patient who has trouble with alcohol.

*Result:* Violent maladaptive behaviors occur with much greater frequency in those who drink excessively, and must be looked for in this group of patients. If a thorough evaluation is not undertaken, the therapist runs the risk of missing other dangerous behaviors in his or her patients.

*Action:* Only see the patient and no one else, in spite of the fact that the patient is intoxicated.

*Result:* Patients who are intoxicated are by definition unreliable historians and may, for example, be contemplating suicide. Therefore, information must be pursued elsewhere. As with any psychiatric emergency, as many sources as possible should be contacted in order to get the most complete picture. Even then difficulties may be overlooked; problems with alcoholics are minimized if others are fed up with them, are ashamed, or just are not aware of the full picture.

*Action:* Ignore the possibility that the alcoholic is self-medicating an underlying psychiatric disorder.

*Result:* Disorders of mood, manic-depressive illness, and recurrent depressions may be missed. The presence of schizophrenia or character disorders are also not rare in this group, and alcohol in combination with these illnesses makes impulsive and self-destructive behavior more likely. If these ill-

81

nesses are missed, then so is an opportunity to offer the patient a less dangerous and more effective treatment for them.

*Action:* Agree that the underlying psychological causes for the patient's alcohol abuse must be uncovered before drinking can cease.

*Result:* The first goal of any treatment is to achieve some degree of sobriety. Waiting for causes to be discovered is usually a rationalization to continue drinking and will likely stymie treatment. Insight can be extremely useful but only after alcohol consumption is curtailed. An intoxicated patient may come up with many "relevant" and "deep" insights only to forget them the next minute.

## Helpful Emergency Interventions

The patient can be evaluated only when sober. If detoxification from alcohol is being considered, the patient must be asked about a prior history of withdrawal syndromes (DT's, withdrawal seizures), since if they happened once they are likely to recur. Detoxification can take place at home or in nonmedical detoxification centers if the patient gives no history of previous, severe withdrawal states and is in good physical health. Otherwise, close medical supervision may be necessary while the patient dries out. After the patient is alcohol-free, the presence of underlying psychiatric disorders will become more obvious.

Attempts should be made to delineate the circumstances when the patient feels compelled to drink. What feelings does the patient have difficulties with? What are the problems that the patient is trying to solve with alcohol? As one patient with underlying manic-depressive illness said: "When I am high I drink to celebrate something. When I am low I drink to forget something." This patient tried to bind with alcohol the agitation associated with both the highs and lows of her disease.

Since alcohol is intimately involved with other maladaptive,

82

destructive behaviors, their possible presence should not be overlooked. At times families suffer from multiple maladaptive states and are involved with a panoply of difficulties— each making further maladaptive behaviors more likely:

A fourteen-year-old cheerleader was brought to the hospital following her third unsuccessful suicide attempt. She had been placed with child welfare on two occasions—after it was revealed that her brothers had intercourse with her, and again when her father sexually molested her—and had just been returned to her family again. Sexual relations had resumed as soon as she moved home. Her father, a high-school counselor, described his sons as "red-blooded American boys" and said he couldn't control them when "they had a few beers in them."

Further evaluation of the case revealed that both boys had recurrent problems with alcohol and one had just lost his license for driving while intoxicated. The father was also a binge drinker who had been told that his liver was already affected by alcohol. Everyone in the family was depressed, three members were problem drinkers, all were involved with incest, and one was actively suicidal. The problems were so ingrained in this family that the daughter was again removed from the home and the father placed in a court-ordered alcohol treatment program.

After the acute medical, social, and psychological issues are attended to, the patient's treatment has just begun. Abstinence is the primary goal of any treatment, but this cannot be achieved unless the alcoholic is clear that he *does* drink. Only after sobriety is achieved can the medical and social disruption caused by the alcohol be attended to and the patient reintegrated into a productive social existence. Family and friends may also need to seek treatment to recover from the disruption.

Patients can expect to feel irritable and have difficulty

sleeping for some time following the cessation of drinking. Physically the central nervous system takes two to three months to fully recover from the effects of alcohol after chronic abuse. Limited prescription for tranquilizers is useful during this period if its use is well monitored. However, pharmacotherapy (besides Antabuse) should not be relied on in the treatment of alcoholics.

The treatment of alcoholism can be greatly enhanced if patient and family become involved in self-help groups such as A.A., particularly if the patient finds groups helpful and is not put off by the spiritual approach of A.A. A.A. now has over one million members. Both private and public agencies provide other types of alcohol treatment services, groups, halfway houses and outpatient clinics. Recently, private corporations have developed nationwide in- and outpatient treatment programs.

There is continued debate about the efficacy of the various forms of alcohol treatment. Some studies indicate that outpatient treatment is as successful as residential care. Others claim that psychotherapy is as helpful as Antabuse. Some experts wonder whether treatment really makes any difference at all—at least when examining large populations. Rather, they say that alcoholism, like any illness, comes in mild and severe forms; those afflicted with the former tend to recover, while the latter don't. What can be unequivocally stated, however, is that family and friends can be helped and that the possibilities of the other dangerous behaviors can be reduced. To repeat: while treatment (or nontreatment) takes place, family and friends must protect themselves—even if this means leaving the alcoholic temporarily or permanently. Spouses and friends must also wonder what caused them to subject themselves to such punishment for so long. Ultimately they must give themselves permission to live their own lives whether or not the alcoholic recovers.

# 3

# Child Abuse, Physical and Emotional Neglect

> All the vicious are vicious through two most involuntary causes, which we shall always ascribe rather to the planter, than the things planted; and to the trainers, rather than those trained.
>
> *Plato*

Child abuse and neglect has a long history. At various times, children have been killed and injured for diverse reasons. They have been sacrificed for religious purposes or murdered for reasons of economics or survival. Until recently, children had few rights; they were treated as chattel. Abuse has moral and religious roots as well. For example, child mistreatment was defended on the grounds that "to spare the rod was to spoil the child."

Historical and social underpinnings of abuse should not be confused, however, with the parental defects in attachment behavior that are central to present-day abuse. Child abuse and neglect, as we know it, results not so much from economic or social factors, but because mothers and fathers are unable to assume or maintain parental roles because of their own problematic early development. Cultural attitudes may have an influence, but the systematic humiliation of children, making them feel unloved and bad, and the commission of violence and torture cannot be blamed on culture and history.

The terms abuse and neglect cover a range of interactions, from "hard-core" physical abuse and murder to more subtle emotional denigration and neglect. We all have read about or know of examples of physical abuse, but emotional abuse and neglect is equally devastating and occurs more frequently. It is the common denominator in all forms of abuse, as here: A four-year-old boy was involved with a puzzle when his father said, "I couldn't do it, your older brother can't do it; what makes you think that you can do it?"

Such verbal attacks may alternate with emotional neglect, as in the case of an eleven-year-old girl who told her teacher that her mother locked her out of the house until five o'clock in the afternoon. "She says she needs time to herself; after that I am allowed in."

In other cases, a seeming lack of concern may mask a basic antipathy toward the child that can lead to injury or tragedy:

A four-year-old wheeled his infant sister's stroller through a department store, repeatedly banging it into the walls. After the baby was dumped onto the floor, the child's mother appeared, put the baby back in her seat, and left. The brother resumed smashing his sister into the wall.

A teacher put her six-month-old and one-and-a-half-year-old child in a bathtub, turned on the water, and left the room to answer the phone. The younger child was severely scalded and died the next day.

Actual physical violence need not be present for severe and lasting damage to ensue. The Apocrypha noted this: "The blow of a whip raises a welt, but a blow of the tongue crushes

bones." A belittling, critical, unloving, and denigrating attitude is often hidden under the veneer of normal family life.
Early emotional neglect may result in failure to thrive; the
child eats poorly and fails to develop normally. If no intervention occurs, the child may die. Thus, the noxious agent is emotional neglect, although the physical aspects of child abuse
may be more visible and immediately lethal.

The variations on the theme of child abuse and neglect are
endless. The statistics are misleading and unrealistically low.
At least 2,000 deaths per year are a direct result of child abuse.
There are thought to be well over 500,000 new cases of physical assault of children each year. Countless more are emotionally neglected.

Within an emotionally neglectful matrix, the actual physical abuse is carried out by whomever has access to the child.
Most abuse is committed by the child's caretaker; mothers'
boyfriends account for 5 percent of abuse, babysitters for 4
percent, and siblings for 1 percent. The rest is parental. Collusion between husband and wife is usual in the mistreatment
of children. It is a rare spouse who is totally unaware of what
the other is doing. This is especially true since potentially abusive men and women tend to marry people with similar problems and backgrounds. Once abuse of one child occurs, there
is a 20 percent chance that a sibling is concurrently being
abused and a 50 percent chance that there is a history of abuse
or that abuse will recur in the future.

Child abuse and neglect occurs in all social strata and in all
educational groups. Among groups of lower economic status,
child abuse is more visible and is more likely to be reported.
Patients from these groups typically receive their medical care
in public agencies, while middle- and upper-class patients
receive medical care from private physicians who are less likely
to identify or report such cases. Also, evidence of abuse and
neglect can be more subtle in privileged groups.

There are many reasons for incorrect and inadequate
reporting. Cases are missed by teachers, pediatricians, and
other health professionals—even though ample indications of

trouble exist. Family and friends overlook evidence because of their discomfort with the subject. They don't know what to look for or what to do when their suspicions are raised. The bottom line is, people don't want to find what, too often, is there.

## THE PARENTAL STANCE:
## ROLE REVERSAL

People have definite styles of parenting. At times parents are more, and at times less, empathic toward their children. Some parents vary widely in their behavior, others are more consistent.

The parents' own childhood experience is the major determinant of what sort of parents they will be. In general, if parents felt loved when young, they will become loving parents themselves. Other circumstances—financial, health status, living circumstances, the presence of a supportive social group, the innate endowment of the child—also influence the parent-child relationship.

What are the characteristics of abusive parents? Some are overtly aggressive, others are docile and overly compliant; interestingly, these are two traits seen early in the development of abused children. Many of the parents are themselves childish: needy and emotionally brittle. These people have rigid and high expectations for their children, expectations that are often not age appropriate. Thus, abuse frequently occurs in response to minor "infractions" such as bedwetting or thumb sucking. Children are expected to be "perfect little ladies and gentlemen" and "know right from wrong" at unrealistically early ages.

The immaturity and self-involvement of these parents can be quite subtle. For instance:

Following an argument with her seven-year-old son on the son's birthday, a mother suddenly left the house in order to "settle down." She did not understand why the child was so upset when she returned, even though she had left the child alone for close to an hour.

Such parents treat children as things rather than people. They give elaborate rationalizations for behavior that has, as its basis, a lack of true empathic understanding for their children. They may allow children to stay home alone at a very early age in order to develop "independence." They may demand that children not cry when sad or hurt in order to encourage "toughness." They may have a young child care for a younger sibling in order to be a "big boy or girl." Many of these children are dressed inappropriately. Little girls may be miniskirted and booted altogether too seductively for their age. These children may also come home from school to an empty house. They are forced by their parents to become independent too early. For example:

An intelligent, hard-working medical resident left her ten-year-old "precociously mature" son home alone when she was on-call every four to seven nights. She was gone all night but saw nothing wrong with this, saying that he was "old for his age," that he could "take care of himself."

The needs of such abusive and neglectful parents take precedence over those of their children. The behavior may be grossly obvious, such as when a small child cares for an alcoholic parent. It may be more covert and rationalized, as with this ten-year-old child. The warping of the parent-child relationship goes even further. Abuse-prone or neglectful parents compete with their children; some children are treated as if they were their parents' siblings and are seen as a source of emotional support.

In fact, role reversal, where the parent inappropriately looks to the child for care, is a major characteristic of child abuse. Such parents want from their children the love that they didn't get from their own parents. Children are asked to parent the

89

parents. They learn at an early age to become the "little man or woman" of the house; to be attentive to their parents' needs. Many abused and neglected children, while compliant and eager to please on the surface, are incapable of entering into truly intimate relationships with their parents or anyone else. Such problems may remain veiled until they become parents themselves. Since these children are taught to be keenly aware of their parents' needs, they rarely know what they are experiencing themselves; their sense of who they are is never firm. They do not have a good idea of self; they exist for the needs of others.

In severe cases, parental motivations for having children give ample clues to the pathological quality of this reversal in the parent-child relationship: "I was lonely," "I only feel good when I'm pregnant," "I wanted someone to need me," "I wanted someone to care for me when I got older." When the child cries or indicates displeasure or independence, these parents, both men and women, feel rejected, hurt, and attacked by their offspring. They will counterattack even though their "tormentors" may be mere infants. The major prerequisites for abuse, then, are an unrealistic appraisal of what a child is and needs, as well as a defect in parental attachment. A gross example of this defect and some clues to the genesis of its existence are found in the following:

A social worker noted that during Faithful's stay in the hospital, Dee, Faithful's mother, also stayed in the hospital "because she had nowhere else to go." Faithful was admitted at age five-and-a-half weeks because she had gained so little weight since birth.

The public health nurse who brought mother and child to the hospital had been trying to get in touch with the mother since a neighbor reported that Dee was seen hitchhiking with Faithful, and that the baby didn't look healthy. When the nurse finally found them at home the baby was cold, lethargic, and weak. The door was wide open, even though it was winter, and the baby was dressed only in diapers, while Dee wore a sweater. The baby was too weak to cry. Dee said the baby hadn't been eating well for a week. She was unaware that Faith was cold, since she herself was hot. On the way to the hospital, the baby somehow fell to the floor of the car while the visiting nurse was not watching.

Dee's own history was revealed in bits and pieces. At age nine she was told by her mother that her aunt was her "real" mother. At fourteen Dee got into trouble at school because she wouldn't change into a gym suit in front of the other girls. She did not want anyone to see the marks that were on her back and legs. She was then sent to the principal, who discovered the bruises. "You could get your parents for child abuse because of this," Dee was told. However, she felt the beatings were "deserved" and wanted to forget all about it. The school did not take any action.

Some early memories that Dee reported were of her "dog being poisoned by a neighbor and falling off her tricycle at age three." She remembered crying to her mother, who said, "I'm busy."

Dee said that as a child she was hit with belts and sticks. Once she remembered being punched in the head by her mother and being left alone with an eight-year-old babysitter all night. When she was a teen-ager, her parents allowed her to babysit for others until "3:30 in the morning," without checking where she was.

Dee felt that she was "spoiled" as a child and "well taken care of." "All I had to do to get anything was to cry." She had no explanation why she was later disowned by her parents or why she never felt close to them.

She began running away from home at a young age and was married for two months at sixteen. Before leaving home for good, she worked with her mother, who cared for foster children. Up to twelve children were in her home at any one time. Dee's mother was a foster mother while she was abusing Dee. Dee did not say whether her mother also beat the other children.

Dee got pregnant at age seventeen and then left home for good. She said that she was "overwhelmed with happiness" when she found out that she was pregnant. The pregnancy was difficult and Dee thought the baby was "nasty" because of "all the kicking"; that "the baby was angry at me while she was inside." However, Dee also said that it was nice to have someone who "needed" her and someone who could take care of her. However, once the baby was born, she had the feeling that the child "did not like" her. But, she said, "the baby is the only thing I got."

Soon after she left the hospital, Dee moved into a group home. There she almost smothered Faithful by leaving a stack of diapers on the edge of the crib. Someone else discovered that the pile of diapers had covered the baby's face, head, and body, and that the child was unable to move and barely able to breathe.

In the hospital it was apparent that Dee was unable to care adequately for the child, and foster placement was arranged. When she was informed of this decision, Dee took Faithful into the women's room and wouldn't come out for over three hours. Finally, she turned the baby over to the hospital social worker and entered a treatment program that was designed to help her regain custody of Faithful.

However, shortly after Faithful was placed, Dee left the state. A few months later she sent a letter to her social worker saying that since she was pregnant again she would no longer be able to care for Faithful and wanted to give her up "for good."

Faithful was placed with an adoptive family when she was ten months old. She had gained weight and was described by a social worker as "adorable, active, and bright."

Two months later the child was brought to a hospital, dead, from multiple skull fractures. Initially, the injuries were said to be "accidental." Apparently Faithful wouldn't "stay still" while her adoptive mother tried to change her diaper. Later it was learned that this mother, too, had been abused as a child.

Abuse begets abuse—violence begets violence. Abusive parents are therefore both victims and culprits; they are simply one part of the generational cycle of abuse and neglect. They are passing on the culture of poor parenting and violence. Faithful's grandmother was abusive and her mother's immaturity and poor parenting skills were obvious. Dee was unable to relate to Faithful in any meaningful way and was usually unaware of the needs of her child. Not noticing that the infant was cold, since she herself was hot, was one example of this lack of empathic awareness. But she was repeating her own experience when young.

This case illustrates another tragic aspect of abuse: the compounding of difficulties by the very system that is supposed to help. Abusive behavior is not infrequently found in foster families or in other institutions. Some child protection agencies are so understaffed and undertrained that they are unable to monitor their placements effectively. Faithful was given to a mother who was herself abused, a fact that became apparent only after Faithful's death.

## THE ABUSIVE CRISIS

C. Henry Kempe and Brandt F. Steele, pioneers in the field, have identified three ingredients necessary for abuse to occur: a child who is seen as different or "bad" and as a cause of parental distress; potentially abusive parents; and stress, which heats up the atmosphere and precipitates the actual abuse. The critical threshold beyond which abuse occurs varies in each family. If the parents' adjustment is poor they may be

93

swamped by the exigencies of everyday life. In such circumstances, minor sources of stress can be lethal, as the following case illustrates:

A twenty-eight-year-old mother, whose three-and-a-half-year-old son had chronic ear infections, felt at her "wit's end" when the television broke. Her child, who spent most of his day watching TV, began insisting on more attention from his mother. At first she tried to comply with his demands but soon became frustrated. She then locked him in his room. When he continued to cry, she punched him in the head, rupturing his eardrum.

Abusive parents experience their children's misbehavior as a reflection of their own worth and as a personal attack. This supersensitivity to perceived criticism precipitates abuse. And many such parents are convinced of the correctness of their approach. Their predicament is that they know of no other way to act. Anything that threatens their self-esteem, no matter how minor, can evoke violence. Verbal or physical violence is resorted to in order to alleviate feelings of helplessness and humiliation. Abuse, then, represents a desperate attempt to reestablish mastery over a situation that feels totally out of control, to undo feelings of humiliation, rejection, and defeat at the hands of a child.

Families with a history of substance abuse (alcoholism, drug abuse), severe emotional illness, chronic physical illness, mental retardation, antisocial behavior, very young parents, a difficult or sick baby, or a past history of child neglect or abuse are at a much higher risk than others for abuse and neglect. The personality and biological attributes of the child are also important. An "easy" baby is less a source of stress than one who may be cranky and less responsive to the parents' ministrations. An "easy" child, therefore, is less likely to be abused. A sick child, on the other hand, will be more at risk. The key factor, however, is that parents tend to repeat what they themselves experienced as children. If they were severely abused as children, they are at risk to repeat this experience no matter how "easy" their baby is in reality.

Different degrees of abuse and neglect can be found at various times in the same family. During periods of high stress—such as illness, divorce, financial setbacks—marginal parents can become severe abusers. Parents who are more "normal" might become neglectful under these circumstances. Thus, the better the adjustment, the more profound the stress necessary to provoke actual abuse. Depending on the circumstances, all parents can be abusive and neglectful. For some, however, abusive behavior is anomalous and out of character, as is seen in the following:

A twenty-four-year-old graduate student and mother of two girls was going through divorce proceedings. She lived in a town where she had few friends and no family. Her father had died two years before and, in addition, her eldest daughter had a seizure disorder. This child had tantrums every time the mother left her alone. During one episode, the mother threw her against the wall, bruising her but causing no serious injuries, severely frightening herself and the child.

This mother's social isolation, divorce proceedings, and sick child precipitated an outburst of violence. However, the abusive threshold was much higher in this woman than in more marginally adjusted parents. Under normal circumstances she was a good enough mother.

## MIDDLE-CLASS ABUSE
## THE DENIAL OF DANGER

Middle-class abuse is often hidden by conventional behavior such as sending children away to boarding school at an early age, spending little time with them, and rarely attending to their emotional needs. A succession of nursemaids might hide a mother's antipathy toward her child. Sending a young child to camp may be the result of a wish to get rid of the child. Parents may shower children with material goods while ignoring their emotional needs. Although physical violence is also frequently present, emotional neglect is often disguised as privileged behavior.

Such abuse may be overlooked by health care professionals, family, and friends because of same-class bias. People do not want to find abuse among people like themselves. Spurious explanations that would be cause for further evaluation in less fortunate families are accepted from the more well-to-do. This denial by health providers is illustrated by the following:

Roberta, a seven-week-old infant, was brought to the hospital because a local physician had diagnosed a sub-dural hematoma, a blood clot in the head, which was most likely due to nonaccidental trauma. The parents said the child had "fallen" during a bath. When X-rays were taken and a thorough physical examination was done, the following were found: blood clots on both sides of the brain, blood in the eyes, a skull fracture, a collar bone fracture, and two leg fractures. All were in various stages of healing and thus were thought to have been incurred over a period of time. Both parents denied any knowledge of how these things could have happened. During the evaluation, which lasted a number of weeks, they presented a picture of extreme innocence and were always very friendly and cooperative.

The father, Jerry, was a lawyer. He had worked at his present job for approximately eight months. Although he described his childhood as "lonesome," he denied any history of abuse. His wife, Judy, seemed pleasant, too, but somewhat childlike. She had finished college by the time they had had their first child, Robert. He had died in another state of "a hole in his heart," which was said to be due to a birth defect.

Both parents strongly denied that there was any question of abuse in Robert's death. Hospital records revealed that Robert did indeed have congenital heart disease. However, when he had died he was also noted to have fractures of the collar bone, right arm, and right leg, all in various stages of healing. The parents had explained that Robert was injured when he "rolled off the couch." This excuse had been accepted by the hospital personnel.

When confronted with the similarities between Robert and Roberta, the parents said that both children were "accident prone." Criminal and civil charges were filed. Eventually, Judy admitted "slapping" Roberta "a few times" although Jerry maintained that he knew nothing about it. Both were placed on two years' probation and ordered into psychiatric treatment, which they attended sporadically. When probation was over, they left the state. Judy was pregnant at the time.

Roberta is living in a state home. She is severely retarded, blind, and has poorly controlled seizures that are due to the injuries she received.

Many abusive parents want to be found out. However, this wish is a mixed one—tempered by the certainty that no one is to be trusted, no one will understand their predicament. As with the other maladaptive behaviors, people are ambivalent about their behavior and, at least in part, want to be stopped. Although Robert was brought to many physicians, abuse was not diagnosed until his sister also began to suffer from suspicious injuries. Furthermore, parental collusion is almost always present in child abuse. It was never absolutely certain, for example, who did the actual beating of Robert and Roberta, although Judy admitted slapping her daughter. Since collusion is so common, parents may not be entirely forthcoming about problems at home in spite of ambivalence about such behavior.

Parents rarely confess abuse directly to a friend, family

member, or physician, since they expect not to be helped and are frightened of losing their mate or child. Though many of these people do not want to hurt their children, they can make their distress known in covert ways. Child abusers visit their physicians complaining of various somatic ills that are usually the result of anxiety and depression, or such parents bring their children in because of "minor" problems. Child abuse, secondary to burns, fractures, or other trauma, becomes obvious only upon closer examination. It is up to the health care professional to get beyond typical minor complaints in order to uncover the abuse.

Children younger than six months are unlikely to cause "accidents." Children rarely "hit" or deliberately injure themselves. Abusive parents, like Roberta's, often delay seeking medical care, waiting until days after the trauma occurs. When they do visit a doctor, the parents' explanation usually does not match the child's condition. Falling off a couch or slipping in the bath would not account for the extent of Robert's and Roberta's injuries. Ten percent of children below age five seen in emergency rooms with "accidents" and other trauma are suffering from child abuse. Even if the child's injuries can be legitimately explained, in many situations one has to wonder if the "accident" resulted from negligent parental supervision.

## DISTURBANCES IN ATTACHMENT
## AND BONDING

Defective parental attachment to their children is the central problem in abuse and neglect. Abuse may occur at various times in the child's life, depending on what behaviors parents are able to tolerate. Some parents function adequately when the child is very young and dependent and become abusive only when the child becomes a toddler and begins to separate. Other parents are unable to tolerate their child's sexuality and become abusive when the child reaches puberty.

Attachment behavior begins at the moment parents consider having a child. Fantasies about what the child will be like are determined by the parents' experiences with their own parents. During the pregnancy the parents may feel generally good. They look foward to the baby and pick out names, prepare a room and clothing. Conversely, some mothers feel estranged from the child even before birth. They may "ignore" the pregnancy by not obtaining proper medical care. Some mothers feel attacked by the child: "He was a mean baby, he kicked me so much." Ambivalent parents may choose a ludicrous or odd name or have difficulty choosing one at all. Mothers at risk for abuse tend to experience "problem" pregnancies, are unhappy and depressed. Fathers, too, may feel the same way. Parents at risk have unrealistic expectations for the child or may not want the child, who is experienced as an intruder, a dangerous stranger.

Clear indicators of severe child abuse and neglect can therefore occur in utero or at the time of delivery:

A twenty-four-year-old woman, who didn't "know" she was pregnant, delivered her baby into a toilet. She saw blood and rushed to the hospital without noticing the newborn. Realizing what had happened, the doctors sent an ambulance to the woman's apartment, where the baby was found alive.

Further problems in attachment become obvious soon after children are born:

One woman was asked when she began having difficulty with her child. She answered "Right away—in the delivery room—she looked at me funny and stuck her tongue out at me—she didn't like me at all."

A new mother was having problems feeding her baby and slapped and pinched her daughter's cheek "in order to get her to eat." The mother saw nothing inappropriate about this behavior, even though the child was two days old.

Such parents—including fathers—are unable to relate empathically to their children, who they perceive as alien or noxious beings: "This child is nasty," "He doesn't like me," "He doesn't mind me" are all indications of what the parents think of *themselves*, which in turn is a residue of their own abusive upbringings. Generally, parents see something pleasant when looking into their babies' faces because they unconsciously remember how their own parents looked at them with pleasure. Abusive parents see something different. When they look at their children, they feel accused, demeaned, and attacked. They reexperience memories of how they were parented themselves; their parents looked at them that way.

Disturbances in the mother-child bond are much more common than previously thought. In fact, in 1973 Brandt Steele noted in a speech that "between 20 and 25 percent of mothers are not turned-on to mothering. . . . These mothers are either outrightly negative, or quite indifferent to their new infant. This is true of normal pregnancies. . . . Tragically, many of these non-turned-on mothers never fulfill the prophecy that we often hear: "She'll learn to love her baby in time." They don't "learn to love their baby in time," and often tragic results occur."

Mothering functions are certainly performed by others as well—most certainly including fathers. In fact, the presence of other more empathic siblings, adults, relatives, or nursemaids can go a long way in protecting "unloved" children from the long-term results of emotional—and physical—abuse.

## THE LONG-TERM EFFECTS
## OF ABUSE

Why certain children escape terrible abuse with only minor difficulties raises intriguing questions. Some children are more resistant to stress than others. Certainly biological factors are at work, as well as the play of chance. As already noted, the establishment of good relationships with siblings, grandparents, or friends offers some protection. The timing of the abuse is also important. The earlier and more prolonged it is, the greater the long-term ill effects.

Primary among the many long-term emotional effects of abuse and neglect are problems with violence and intimacy, and an inability to modulate strong feelings. Physical sequelae are also found in severe cases.

Trust in others is built on the foundation of trusting one's parents. Frustration tolerance and the ability to soothe oneself derives from having been adequately comforted as a child. Consequently, abused children feel empty, mistrustful, unlovable, bad, and alone. They have difficulty in experiencing love, happiness, accomplishment, and contentment, since they feel that they deserve to be beaten and neglected. They also have a hard time metabolizing and dealing with feelings and frustration; they may resort to action in order not to experience strong emotion. Their style of relating to others may be indiscriminate, childish, and unreliable. Feeling compelled to please, they form rapid but shallow relationships. They are chronically depressed.

Self-punishment and violence are often present in some form, and for different reasons, in the later lives of abused and neglected children. Since most people who were abused assume that they deserved to be beaten, they continue to hurt themselves, seeking further punishment that they feel they deserved at the hands of a parent. Suicide and self-mutilation—gross examples of such self-destructive behavior—can have this meaning:

A nineteen-year-old man came to an emergency room claiming that a laceration on his leg was caused by an accident. Because of multiple scars on his body, further history was obtained. It was found that when the patient was three, his mother attacked him with a pair of scissors. When he was five, she tried to run him over with a car. At age nine, he began to carve incisions on his own

101

abdomen and arms with a razor. This behavior continued into adult life.

Such behavior also perpetuates the overstimulation that many of these people seem to need, and serves the function of repeating certain aspects of earlier parental relationships. It may also represent an unconscious attempt to master the initial trauma of being attacked while young.

Some victims seem docile and compliant on the surface, but overt sadism plays a large part in the lives of other casualties of abuse. For instance, a history of abuse is found in the majority of murderers and rapists. These behaviors may be an unconscious means of gaining revenge on abusive parents. Identifying with the aggressor, many abused children grow up to be abusive mates and parents.

The tables can be turned more directly; some abused children attack their tormentors. An estimated 1,500–2,000 parents per year are killed by their children, and many more parents are attacked and beaten. It is said that one in ten families with teen-age children experience violence directed toward adults in the home. The following is a serious example of this:

Two children hired a man to murder their father. After his death, the seventeen-year-old son and four-teen-year-daughter hid his body and went on a spending spree using their father's credit cards. "He wouldn't let us smoke pot," the children complained, explaining why they murdered him. The father kept three Bibles in the living room, which he read to his children after severely whipping them every Sunday in order to "drive out sin."

The following nursery rhyme from *Mother Goose* describes the depressed and sadistic later life of three abused children. Problems with violence and the wish for revenge are obvious

102

as is the essentially lonely quality of these peoples' lives: "Tom tied a kettle to the tail of a cat; Jill put a stone in the blind man's hat; Bob threw his grandmother down the stairs—and they all grew up ugly and nobody cares."

Abuse has long-lasting physical effects. Abused children may be blind, spastic, retarded, or otherwise injured. Intellectual impairment can result from physical abuse or physical and emotional neglect. Language and motor development can also be delayed.

## COMMON REACTIONS TO
## CHILD ABUSE

People are instinctively repelled and horrified by child abuse, although the enlightened view is that all parents are potential abusers. Perhaps the strong reactions are due, in part, to discomfort with this latter fact. People don't want to see in others what may be upsetting in themselves. In the last twenty years much attention has been paid to the problem— child protection teams have been formed, laws related to reporting child abuse passed, public educational campaigns mounted. Yet abuse is still grossly under-reported—emotional and physical neglect even more so.

Reactions to the abusive situation will profoundly affect the perpetrators and children. Abusive parents are extremely sensitive to criticism and, if censored, will withdraw from any evaluative or treatment effort. Those who want to help must become aware of, and try to control, their own responses to the abusive situation. Child abuse, by its very nature, evokes strong reactions. An entire range of responses is normal and needs to be acknowledged.

The following are some of the more common responses to child abuse:

1. *Deny* that abuse has occurred or is even possible. The observation of repeated beatings, scaldings, burnings, pinches,

punches, and slaps all have a numbing effect on the observer. "It is so awful that I don't want to think that it exists; therefore it doesn't," seems to be the reasoning here. Emotional neglect and denigration are even more easily overlooked.

Denial short-circuits the anxiety that accompanies an observer's recognition of abuse and identification with the beaten child, the wish to punish the parent, and the realization that the observer may also have fears of violence. Denial also protects the observer from deciding what action to take if abuse is acknowledged.

2. *Experience anger.* The wish to punish the abuser may stem from an identification with the child; the onlooker feels as if he has been attacked by the parent. The observer may, in fact, have been abused or neglected as a child and thus have even more reason for such a strong reaction. By getting angry, the observer is saying, "It is not possible that I will ever act this way!" This person seldom displays empathic understanding for the abusive parent's predicament.

3. *Blame the child for the abuse.* The idea that the child is naughty and deserves punishment can be a reflection of the historical notion that children are inherently bad and should be beaten to ensure moral and upright development. This response minimizes the brutality of the attack, the helplessness of the child, and the inappropriateness of parental expectations. Abusive parents who "punish" an infant for being "nasty" demonstrate a total lack of empathic understanding of children. Toilet training may be a particularly dangerous period for children whose parents need strict obedience from others in order to feel worthwhile themselves.

The blame response is also in concordance with many victims' view of themselves. This poor self-image must be overcome if the victim is to avoid believing that he or she is bad, only to repeat destructive behavior later in life.

4. *Label abuse as a problem of crazy people*—or, if that isn't so, of the less privileged, of the retarded, or of "anyone else but me." This response distances the observer from the possibility

of abuse since it situates abuse in another place and in another mind (not mine).

Mentally ill people who are delusional about their children may, in fact, be particularly dangerous. Psychotic parents may kill or otherwise injure their children for bizarre and weird reasons. However, only 10 percent of abusive parents suffer from severe mental illness. The others are usually not distinguishable from a broad cross-section of the population. The vast majority of abuse and neglect is not of the dramatic, psychotic kind.

5. *Fail to intervene,* since everyone is a potential abuser. This "understanding" reaction is a prescription for trouble. The assumption is that identification of abusive parents is purely a punitive act, not one that will provide help for the parents and children. The observer may be hesitant to "betray" a friend or family member, especially for behavior that is potentially in everyone's repertoire. Even though reporting a case of abuse does not guarantee the child's safety or the immediate amelioration of the abusive situation, abusive families need outside assistance and are usually relieved to be found out. Most abusive families can be helped. Abuse is a treatable problem.

## DANGER SIGNALS
## CLUES TO ABUSE AND NEGLECT

In order for abuse and neglect to be diagnosed properly, a high index of suspicion must be maintained and there must be willingness—by family, friends, and clinicians—to explore the possibility of its existence.

It is useful to divide danger signals and indicators of potential abuse into those found prenatally and those that occur after the child is born. This allows potentially high-risk parents to be identified before delivery and for possible interventions to be planned before the newborn child is in danger.

105

Many of the danger signals that follow are transiently found in normal families and should not be cause for alarm. However, if they persist and more than one or two exists, the possibility for abuse is higher than in the normal population. Most of the clues, even though the list is long, follow from a central defect of bonding and attachment in the parent-child relationship.

*Prenatal danger signals:*

• The parents suffer from a psychotic mental illness, alcohol or drug abuse, or any other condition that would make them unreliable or unable to care for the child.

• An unplanned pregnancy with very young parents.

• A long delay in "realizing" that conception has occurred. Other forms of denial, such as avoiding maternity clothes, may also point to the wish not to have the child.

• Lack of planning for the child; for example, having trouble finding names so that none are chosen by the time of delivery, or not planning for where the child will sleep or preparing clothing or a room.

• Not obtaining, or delaying, adequate prenatal medical care.

• The presence of severe anxiety or depression in either parent during the pregnancy, with a decrease in psychosocial functioning, such as loss of a job or suicidal behavior. Considering an abortion or wishing to relinquish the child during the pregnancy is an ominous sign.

• An increase in "psychosomatic" concerns, by either the mother or father. This is often accompanied by many visits to physicians or clinics.

• Spousal violence, suicide attempts, or other chaotic behaviors, such as alcoholism, drug abuse, or trouble with the law.

• Lack of adequate social supports for the parents such as family or close friends. An inability to turn to anyone for help.

• Lack of understanding about what the child will mean, and what changes will occur in family life. "Things will be as usual" is certainly unrealistic, and may lead to problems in attachment.

*Post-natal clues:*

• Does the parent hold the baby, establish eye contact, call the baby by name, and soothe the baby when it is distressed?

• Does the parent leave the baby in precarious and dangerous positions, such as on top of dressers?

• Does the parent hold and cuddle the baby during feeding or is the baby always propped up in a crib?

• Does the parent make demeaning remarks about the child?

• Does the parent express overconcern with the child's sex, or have high and unrealistic expectations for the baby; for example, the baby will care for me, I know she will be a "perfect child."

• Does the parent display interest in the child or only in himself / herself?

• Does the husband seem jealous of the new baby? Does he criticize how the mother is caring for the baby and how much attention the baby is getting?

• For whom is the child named? Someone who was loved? After an unavailable or abusive parent?

• Does the mother have help with the child? Is she stuck at home with nowhere to go and with no one to help?

• How do the parents feel when the child cries? Inadequate? Frantic? What do they do? Can they comfort the child? Do they feel that the child is trying to "bug" them? Do they seem helpless and always at a loss as to what to do?

• How do the parents respond to the baby's eating, voiding, defecating? Do these functions disgust them?

• Do the parents seem to be having fun with the child? Do they say nice things about the child or are they always critical?

• Do the parents have many physical concerns about the baby? Do they tell highly unlikely stories about the child, such as that he or she stopped breathing for a long period of time? Do they bring the child to many doctors with diverse and sometimes strange complaints?

• Do the parents delay in seeking medical attention? Many abusive parents present complaints that don't fit the child's condition.

• Does the child appear to have frequent accidents or suffer from many scratches, burns, bruises?

• Do the parents visit doctors with multiple somatic, hypochondriacal complaints or seem overly preoccupied with their own health?

• Is the child unkempt, dirty, undernourished, or chronically tired?

• When older, is the child frequently left alone? Does the child appear depressed or, on the other hand, exhibit hostile outbursts against peers? Does the child seem docile and overly compliant?

• Children who are abused will have a higher incidence of behavioral disturbances, such as bedwetting, hyperactivity, school problems, and so forth.

• Among physically or sexually abused adolescents there is high incidence of school problems, trouble with the law, running away, substance abuse, and suicidal behavior.

## WHAT THEY SAY
## WHAT THEY MEAN

Although abusive parents are often relieved to be found out, they try to hide their true situation. The following are some examples of what they may say in order to avoid discovery:

| Says | Means |
|---|---|
| I never have problems with my baby. | I had to leave the house yesterday because I was frightened of strangling the child. |
| He is mature for his age and is very independent. | I have a hard time judging how appropriately to care for my child. I fre- |

| *Says* | *Means* |
|---|---|
| | quently leave him home alone although he is only seven. I don't understand children. |
| I have no idea how these bruises occurred; I think he hit himself. Maybe it was an accident. | I was so upset I couldn't comfort the child. I thought that meant that I am a bad parent, so I hit him. |
| I had no idea that my husband was doing these things. | I am so frightened of being alone that I am afraid that he will leave me if I criticize him. Besides, isn't this the way children should be raised? |
| Things just got out of hand. You know how it is. It won't happen again. | I hope you don't believe this rationalization—but it is very hard for me to tell you how upset I am. |
| Everything would be fine if you would just leave us alone. | I am angry, *but also* relieved to have been discovered. I know we need help but we don't know how to get it. |

## GENERAL APPROACHES
## TO CHILD ABUSE AND NEGLECT

All you have to do is ask the parent
how they are feeling; then sit back
and listen.

*Brandt F. Steele, M.D.*

Abusive parents do not, as a group, want to hurt their children. Of course, there are sadists and sociopaths who abuse, neglect, and exploit children. These people rarely will change their behavior. However, the majority of abusers are able to benefit from treatment that will allow the child to remain in the home and that will, it is hoped, interrupt the transmission of abuse from one generation to the next. The primary obstacle to obtaining treatment for parents and children is inadequate casefinding and reporting; the second is insufficient evaluation of the problem once it becomes known.

## Commonly Made Errors

Before therapeutic interventions can occur, people may try a number of strategies that are less than helpful. The following are some possible maneuvers, what would be the result, and why this result is likely to occur.

*Action:* Ignore the evidence and hope that the abuse or neglect will cease.
*Result:* The immediate danger of abuse may diminish once a family crisis has passed, but it is likely to recur. As mentioned earlier, there is a 20 percent rate of concurrent abuse of other children in the family and a 50 percent chance that abuse has occurred in the past or will happen again. A hands-off approach creates continued danger for children.

*Action:* Express concern to the nonabusive parent.
*Result:* This approach allows the observer to feel less guilty, but the family will not be helped and probably will withdraw. Remember that parental collusion in all kinds of abuse is practically universal. Although the "nonabusive" parent may express shock or dismay, it is highly unlikely that he or she is unaware. It may be difficult to judge who exactly is doing what, and, at times, both parents can be abusers. Such an approach may help the nonabusive parent break through his or her own denial but the case must still be reported to child welfare.

110

*Action:* Tell the child that his parents are having "problems," and that he should attempt to improve his own behavior.

*Result:* Abused children usually feel that they are responsible for their denigration, abuse, and neglect. Telling them to behave will reinforce this pathogenic misperception. Furthermore, children are rarely abused for being "bad" in the commonly accepted sense but rather because of their parents' unrealistic expectations and poor attachment behavior. What the child really needs to hear is that his parents are having problems and that it is *not* his fault.

*Action:* Warn the parents that you will call the police if the abuse doesn't stop.

*Result:* Most abusive parents know that what they are doing is wrong. Those involved in neglect may be less clear about their behavior. However, the majority are mistrustful and do not expect to get help; they are accustomed to threatening and being threatened. They will therefore be convinced that this threat is meant punitively, which it is. Their notion that no real help is possible is supported, and they probably will move away and become even more isolated. Parents should be told that child-abuse agencies are meant to help and not punish.

*Action:* Offer to help the parents with the child or with the chores and other household duties.

*Result:* Although this approach can be extremely helpful in relieving the pressure that leads to abuse and neglect, it is not enough. Attempting to "rescue" the family underestimates the seriousness of most abusive situations. Any parent who is suspected of abuse needs to be evaluated professionally by people trained in such matters. Even if the abuse stops, psychotherapeutic intervention is usually necessary for the depression and low self-esteem present in both parents and children.

111

## Helpful Interventions

Once suspected, abuse and neglect should be professionally evaluated. The only really adequate approach is to notify the local child protective services or welfare agencies of your concern. Reports of suspected abuse will remain confidential. Proof isn't necessary. That is the job of the child protective service workers, physicians, and others who will investigate the report.

Find out the name of the person with whom you register the complaint, and ask the worker to evaluate the problem immediately. If nothing is done, call again. If necessary, call the worker's supervisor. Unfortunately, child protective services vary in adequacy from community to community. The only way they will improve is through increased citizen involvement.

Speaking with overwhelmed and potentially abusive parents can be useful but not in lieu of filing a report. Questions such as: "It must be difficult to work so hard and care for _____," or "Being a parent is tough and can be, at times, very hard" or "It is normal to get frustrated and angry at children when things are not going well" will not be seen as an attack on the parent and will indicate to them that you understand their point of view. Most parents at their wit's end who are abusing or neglecting their children will be grateful, if suspicious, about the offer for help. Reporting the case to child welfare should be presented in this light: as potential for help and not as a punishment.

Offering abusive families help with daily chores, giving the parents a break with the children, can be extremely useful but also not in lieu of a report. These people will initially be mistrustful of most that is offered to them; don't be put off by attempts to sabotage assistance.

Chaotic families may be involved with a number of dangerous behaviors. Suicide of either parent is a definite possibility. Incest may coexist with physical abuse. If the danger of lethal-

112

ity is high, call the police immediately for help, to prevent both active physical abuse and other destructive activities.

## THE MEDICAL EVALUATION
## OF CHILD ABUSE

Child abuse comes to physicians' attention in a number of different ways, in both the office and hospital. When abuse is already suspected, cases will be referred by child protective services for documentation and treatment. Doctors may also see children with unexplained trauma, bruising, failure to thrive—all clues to abuse. As mentioned, abusive parents may complain of vague somatic disturbances that are symptomatic of underlying anxiety or depression. These complaints become unconscious "tickets for admission" to the health care delivery system. Such patients visit doctors and are covertly seeking help for their difficulties at home. For instance, the following patient was relieved to reveal her difficulties:

A young woman, recently divorced and out of work, felt cooped up at home with her six-month-old son and one-and-a-half-year-old daughter. On the morning of admission, she felt at "wit's end"; the children were driving her "crazy." She ground up a lethal dose of sleeping pills and put them in her son's milk bottle. But before he could drink much of it she grabbed the bottle away. Two hours later she appeared in a medical emergency room with complaints of back pain. Because she was unhappy with the suggested treatment, heat and analgesics, she was seen by a psychiatric consultant who obtained the story about her circumstances at home. She gratefully accepted homemaker help and other psychotherapeutic interventions.

Such patients are not consciously trying to deceive their doctors; rather, their physical difficulties are symptomatic of

113

organismic distress. It is up to the physician to get beyond their complaints in order to uncover potentially lethal behavior.

Once abuse is identified, proper medical and psychosocial evaluation of both children and parents is the cornerstone of all successful future treatment. Stress reduction is of immediate concern. Long-term character change is necessary if abuse is not to recur. Before other psychological treatments are planned, however, an expert medical evaluation needs to be undertaken.

The medical evaluation should be done by someone trained in abuse and neglect. Inexperience can be fatal to the child. Consultation should always be sought by the inexperienced examiner. The examination may need to take place in the hospital if the child appears to be injured or if the parents are unreliable or threatening or give a history of previous physical abuse.

Accusatory questioning should obviously be avoided. The assumption of abuse may be incorrect and the parents will become less cooperative if this approach is taken. Cases of suspected abuse should be seen right away and not be kept waiting, even if the injuries are not physically serious. Delay in waiting rooms must be minimized. These cases represent social and psychological, if not medical, emergencies and the parents may leave with the child before being seen.

## Commonly Made Medical Errors

Here are some of the more usual medical errors that are made by physicians unfamiliar with child abuse:

*Action:* Fail to explore the possible presence of abuse in families with marital discord, severe health problems, substance abuse or mental illness, or other symptoms of distress.

*Result:* When the examiner is uncomfortable asking questions or is fearful of uncovering abuse, an opportunity is missed for early intervention. This is particularly true if the physician feels the patient will be insulted by certain inquiries. The doctor may unconsciously ignore clues to abuse, since to find it in others is potentially to find it in oneself.

*Action:* Neglect to perform a thorough physical and laboratory examination.

*Result:* Often, abusive parents will initially deny abuse or will only admit to milder forms. If there is *any* evidence of abuse, the case should be thoroughly studied. Multiple old fractures in various stages of healing can be discovered by X-ray. Injuries may be hidden and hard to find, particularly around the genital region or in the mouth. Retinal hemorrhages exist without obvious external injury. Severe brain damage occurs after violent shaking but with no signs of external trauma. There is no substitute for an adequate, thorough, and meticulous exam.

*Action:* Fail to examine other members of the family, particularly siblings with whom the abuser has been in contact.

*Result:* Abuse runs in families. Even though one child may be singled out and scapegoated, there is a good chance that others are involved in abuse or have been in the past. It is also useful to obtain historical information from as many family members as possible. This is particularly important, since there are often associated difficulties. For example, significant parental or sibling depression may be found and suicide averted because of a complete family examination. The extent of the problem will not be appreciated unless the whole family is evaluated.

## Helpful Medical Interventions

An outline of what comprises a proper medical examination follows here. With such an examination, the majority of injuries can be determined as due to abuse or to accidental causes. A small number of cases will not be clear, and it should also be remembered that severe emotional neglect can occur

115

without physical signs of abuse. A thorough medical exam forms the basis for all further treatment.

• All physical findings should be adequately described and photos taken if possible. Bruises, marks, scratches, burns, and so forth should be listed by size, shape, and color.
• Hidden trauma should be suspected in all cases and therefore bones and joints should be carefully palpated and the eyes, ears, and mouth thoroughly examined.
• Look for injuries in various stages of healing: bite and strap marks, bruises, burns, fractures, scars.
• Examine the usual areas of trauma: the lower back, buttocks, genitals, inner thighs, cheeks, and earlobes. Half of physically abused children sustain injuries to the face and mouth. For example, jamming a bottle into a baby's mouth may cause bruises of the upper lip and the tongue. Oval bruises anywhere on the body are usually due to hand and grasp marks. Objects such as belt buckles or brushes leave characteristic marks.
• Ten percent of abuse is by burning. The usual places that are injured are the palms, soles, or abdomen. Parents may burn the child's hands as punishment for touching forbidden objects and scald a child's buttocks in hot water if the child has difficulty with toilet training. Other burns are inflicted by such instruments as lighters, cigarettes, and hot pokers.
• Subdural hematomas (bleeding in the skull) may result from violent shaking of the child. Such injuries may develop slowly, and their presence should always be suspected. The child may not show any external signs of trauma.
• Failure to thrive or to grow adequately may be due to abuse and neglect. It is thought that failure to thrive is due 30 percent to occult physical disease, 20 percent to feeding error, and 50 percent to neglect. Neglect is almost a certainty if a child begins to gain weight while in the hospital and does not do so at home.
• All abused children under age five should be X-rayed for fractures. Blood screens in children whose parents claim that they bruise or bleed easily should also be obtained. Children

116

CHILD ABUSE

under six months of age, no matter what the parental explanation for trauma, *must* be considered to be victims of abuse. These are the children who, when sent home prematurely, are brought back dead.

• If the child is to be treated as an outpatient during the abusive crisis, there should be at least *one examination per week in the doctor's office*. After the crisis has passed, regular checkups should be arranged in conjunction with the child protection agency and/or other mental health professionals involved with the family's care.

• If the child needs to be hospitalized and the parents are unwilling, emergency police holds and court orders should be obtained. Children *should not be allowed* to return home if a chance of immediate physical abuse is suspected or if there is a good chance that the family is unreliable and will be lost to follow-up.

## EMERGENCY PSYCHIATRIC INTERVENTIONS

Concurrent with the medical evaluation of the child and family, an extensive psychosocial evaluation is necessary. A past history that focuses on the risk factors of abuse must be obtained from as many sources as possible. The clinical interview is also a good tool in judging such emotional difficulties.

Throughout, therapists should avoid a judgmental-critical stance, since parents certainly will not reveal the true state of affairs to someone they view as punitive. There are some clinicians who *should not be involved with abuse cases,* since they are unable to adopt this attitude.

### Commonly Made Psychiatric Errors

*Action:* Fail to get information from as many sources as possible: family, friends, health or child protective agencies, past medical records, and other physicians.

117

*Result:* An adequate evaluation takes time and effort. Abusive parents are likely to move frequently. To make matters worse, they obtain medical care in many different places and often do not keep follow-up appointments. Thus, a suspicious injury or death in another state may be overlooked if this information is not tracked down. Patterns of family disorganization and abuse will become obvious only after meticulous examination. Shortcuts can be dangerous and are the cause for most medical mistakes.

*Action:* Use euphemisms when talking with parents or children, thus avoiding direct questions about abuse.
*Result:* Most clinicians are uncomfortable asking about the extent of the abuse. If the therapist is upset by such details, the intensity of the problem cannot be appreciated. Avoidance of direct questioning also reveals the therapist's discomfort to the parents. Parents then feel even less secure with the therapist and more ashamed of what is going on.

*Action:* Assume the danger of abuse is over when abusive parents seem cooperative during the interview.
*Result:*. Superficial compliance of abusive parents can resemble real change and hide continued abuse. Abusive parents are quick to sense what is expected of them and to conform, a survival skill learned as children at the hands of their own parents. These shifts in behavior may be opportunistic and unreliable and cannot be counted on.

*Action:* Cease the psychotherapeutic treatment of the abused child when the physical abuse ceases or when the child is placed in a safe environment.
*Result:* A well-known but overlooked fact is that abused children suffer from many long-term psychological, behavioral, and developmental difficulties that frequently are ignored by mental health professionals once the physical danger has passed. Such children continue to experience problems with self-esteem, aggression, and depression.

Furthermore, children, if they are separated from their parents, no matter how abusive, become depressed and will have to grieve their loss. Treatment of these children should continue even after the danger of physical violence is over.

## Helpful Emergency Intervention

The goals of emergency psychiatric treatment are: 1) to physically protect the child; 2) to protect the parents from their destructive impulses; 3) to identify the immediate sources of stress that are triggering the abusive behavior; and 4) to help to create a therapeutic environment so that the parent-child relationship can begin to normalize.

The clinical interview is designed to evaluate realistically how the parents view the child and to ascertain the presence of neglect or actual abuse. During this interview, the parents must be examined for the presence of psychiatric disorders, which increase the probability of neglect and increase the possibility of lethality. Any psychotic illness, severe depression, or substance abuse (alcohol and other drugs) is particularly ominous. Alcoholism in either parent may make it impossible for the child to be cared for at home so long as the parent is drinking. Parents may be delusional about their children. They may project onto their children their own poor self-images, and then view their children as "devils" or "sinners." The parents then punish a projection of their own badness, thus reenacting punishment at the hands of their own parents. Here is an extreme example of what can result if the parent is psychotic:

A twenty-year-old mother was found in the front seat of her car with her daughter after she had cut her child's heart out. The mother, who thought that the child was the devil, said that she, the mother, was "trying to save the world."

During the examination, parents should be seen in a quiet room and the interview conducted in an unhurried way. The

119

parents may be set at ease if the clinician says he would like to see if he can help the parents or their children. If the parents ask about the exact purpose of the interview, the suspicion of abuse should not be denied. Otherwise, the area of abuse should be eased into slowly. It is helpful initially to focus on the child or children so that parents do not feel attacked or demeaned. Questions such as "Are your children hard to manage?" or "Is it difficult to get your children to obey you?" will show parents that the evaluation is meant to be helpful.

The quality of the relationship between the parent and the child will become apparent to the skilled interviewer. If the children are old enough to talk—past age three—they should be interviewed without the parents, either verbally or in play therapy session(s). Children may be frank about what has been going on, although they may also deny the abuse if they have already "bought into" the family's distorted relationships, feel that they deserve punishment, and are frightened or are fearful of betraying the family.

These questions will be helpful: "Who is at home when you go to sleep?" "Do you eat breakfast, lunch, and dinner?" "Who fixes your meals?" Questions about physical abuse can be asked directly—for example, "Who punishes you?" "How?" "Are you hit or burned?" and so forth. A nonjudgmental approach here is crucial, since the child will feel emotionally attached to his or her abuser.

The following are some areas it will be useful to explore with the parents when abuse is suspected:

• How was the pregnancy experienced? Was the mother ill most of the time? Did she get depressed after the delivery? Was there any spousal violence or other marital discord during the pregnancy? Was the child planned? Was a name chosen and a room picked out ahead of time? What was the delivery like? These questions will help in understanding the parents' readiness to bond to the child.

• What did the parents expect the child to be like? A monster? A companion? Both are inappropriate expectations if they are the primary views of the child.

• Do the parents feel that their child is purposely trying to provoke them? This feeling is especially revealing if the answer is yes and the abused child is an infant. Older children may in fact become extremely provocative and heighten the danger.

• At what age do the parents think the child knows right from wrong? When would the parents punish the child? At six months? At one year? These questions will uncover unrealistic ideas about children and reveal *overly perfectionistic views* of what children ought to be like.

• Who does the babysitting? Does a young sibling care for a smaller child? At what age do the parents feel they can leave the child alone? At what age is the child sent away to camp? To school?

• Do the parents spend time playing with the child? How many hours does the child spend in front of the television? Does the family do things together? Do the parents spend most of their vacation time away from the child?

• How do the parents feel when the child cries? What do they do? Do they have to leave the room or the house to avoid hurting the child? Do they feel overwhelmed with responsibility for the child? (A negative answer to this question would be worrisome—a certain amount of feeling overburdened is common among normal parents.)

• Do the parents have someone to call on for help with the child—can they get away for awhile? Do they feel justified in asking for help? Most abusive parents do not.

• Do the parents ever have thoughts of hurting the child? A positive answer might be considered normal. A strong denial is cause for alarm. Most parents have occasionally been driven to distraction by a crying baby they have been unable to soothe. Acting on this impulse, however, is another matter.

• Do the parents ever get so frustrated with the children that they punish them? Who does this? How? With what methods? Does the parent use a strap or a switch? Does the parent ever leave welts, bruises, or marks? Has the parent ever been frightened of killing the child? Specifics are important.

The causes of the current abusive crisis should be elucidated and the chances of further maladaptive behavior decreased. When the causes of abuse are uncovered, the patient may be able to deal with these sources of stress more effectively, as happened in the following cases:

A high-school principal would humiliate and denigrate his son by calling him a "wimp" and "candy-ass" whenever he himself felt devalued at work. After the father became aware of this connection, he attempted to cease castigating his son.

An army captain severely beat his two daughters, particularly when he felt that his children did not show him the proper respect. It became clear, however, that these beatings occurred more frequently if he felt that his wife and children were going to leave him. He was terrified of being alone and his abusive behavior represented maladaptive attempts to hold his family together. When he realized this, the behavior ameliorated to some degree, but eventually the family had to separate.

These two cases indicate pervasive problems with fears of devaluation, humiliation, and loss. Such problems of parental self-esteem must be the focus of longer-term psychotherapeutic work with abusive parents.

If the parent is found to be psychotic, is unable to control himself or herself, or has a poor history of treatment compliance, emergency hospitalization or foster placement of the child and siblings should be considered, along with psychiatric hospitalization of the parent. The "nonabusive" parent may also be unreliable, since collusion between parents is usually the case in all forms of abuse and neglect. At times the only way these parents will actively stay in therapy is through court-ordered, long-term supervision and treatment.

Therapists must be prepared to be tested and provoked and must be available in crisis situations. Some parents will be slow to trust but will make good use of the help after a reasonable relationship is established. One mother eventually was able to establish a useful and sound therapeutic relationship:

Initially she became easily overwhelmed when her child demanded attention and care. She resorted to severe punishment of the child, locking him in his room so that she would not "kill him." During the early phases of treatment, she was encouraged to call the child protection team when these destructive urges occurred. A team member would then make a home visit, sometimes in the early morning hours, to help buffer the mother from acting on further abuse. Eventually she was able to internalize these controls and take them as her own. She was then better able to tolerate her child's demands and not resort to abusive behavior when under stress.

Child abuse treatment often requires a team approach. One therapist is rarely enough. Coordination among treatment personnel is crucial. Some parents do well in support groups such as Parents Anonymous. Lay therapists, homemakers, and visiting nurses have all proven useful. Parenting skills classes can also bolster parents' confidence and increase their self-esteem, thus reducing the danger of abuse.

Foster home placement must be considered if the situation remains dangerous in spite of interventions. Most abusive parents appear to be devastated when placement is considered. However, many are ultimately relieved; sad and depressed about the separation, they will also be unburdened. Foster placement may be temporary, allowing time for the abusive family to get help; or it may occur following the permanent termination of parental rights. In either case, long-term psychotherapeutic work with abused children should continue.

Help from multiple agencies can be called in, often before abuse has become severe. But some families are left unsupervised, and these cases fall between the cracks because of jurisdictional or "administrative" disputes. Someone must be put in charge of the cases; otherwise overwhelmed families overwhelm the system and get lost to follow-up.

Older victims of child abuse, and adults who were abused during childhood, can also benefit from psychotherapeutic work focusing on issues of self-esteem, depression, impulse control, and problems with intimacy. One young man was not able to enter college until during psychotherapy he overcame the conviction that his father would devalue his efforts if he were alive. A young woman found it impossible to become intimate with a man because she was frightened of being overwhelmed by his demands for care and fealty, and for fear of betraying her mother. Her "job" as a child had been to care for her alcoholic mother, who became intensely jealous when she made moves toward independence. The young woman worried that her boyfriend would do the same. She was able to resolve these issues and now has a family of her own.

Abuse and neglect result from multiple factors. Any treatment approach must take into account intrapsychic, social, economic, and cultural influences. If the treatment focuses only on one thing—for example, housing or economic factors—it will be unsuccessful. A broad-based team approach is most likely to succeed. Adult victims of abuse who are identified and offered psychotherapeutic help may be able to undo destructive patterns learned when young.

# 4

# Father-Daughter Incest

> When I told my mother that my
> father was bothering me, she called
> me a liar.
>
> *A victim*

> I couldn't sing "Happy Birthday"
> to myself because I thought I didn't
> deserve it.
>
> *A victim*

Incest is defined as any sexual event between relatives who
are not allowed by law to marry. This chapter will discuss incest
perpetrated on a child by a family member. A father, an uncle,
or brother may be having sexual contact with a female or male
child relative. Occasionally, homosexual and heterosexual
incest coexist. For example, a two-year-old girl was abused by
her mother as well as by her mother's boyfriend. The latter
situation, although considered sexual abuse, is not actually
incest, since the offender and victim were not related.

The most frequently reported cases of incest occur between
father and daughter. Sibling incest is probably more common

but is said to be less emotionally damaging because of its transient nature, unless one partner is viewed as parental by virtue of age or status, or if the incest progresses beyond petting. Homosexual incest—once said to be extremely rare—is being reported with greater frequency. Another form of incest— where the incest taboo is sometimes diluted—is between stepchild and stepparent. This Phaedra complex can still have profoundly damaging psychological consequences for the child, particularly since the dynamics here are often similar to those found in cases of father-daughter incest.

Why mother-son incest is so rare—if it is—is open to debate. The taboo against this form seems stronger than against some of the others. Perhaps women control themselves better than men, are more self-contained and less impulsive. Therefore, when under stress, women are more likely to get depressed, while men are more likely to resort to action. Women at risk— those raised in abusive environments—may be more depressed and sexually repressed than their male counterparts and hence do not repeat their experiences directly. Rather, they are prone to marry men who will sexually abuse their daughters. Perhaps, too, such women turn elsewhere, out of the home, for emotional gratification and establish capacities and outlets not available to men. Women seem to be more able to get emotional support from other women than men are able to get from men. Men seem more easily isolated. Thus, women may be less likely to act destructively, at least in this arena. There may be other differences. Little girls seem more sexually advanced than little boys—at least in our culture. Incestuous fathers say that they are able to fantasize that they are with women when they are with their daughters; it seems that mothers would be hard pressed to say this when with their sons, at least before puberty. When mother-son incest is reported, a number of factors are usually found: the mother was absent during the child's formative years, severe alcoholism or other psychopathology is present in the mother or child, and a strong family history of incest is discovered. However, it would not be surprising if with improved reporting the disparity between types were reduced. Knowledge of incest is where information about child abuse was in the 1960s. For the moment, most is known about father (and stepfather)-daughter incest, and that aspect of the behavior forms the basis of this chapter. Many of the points discussed will be useful in understanding other forms of incest as well.

Incestuous activity can range from one episode of fondling between say, a grandfather and granddaughter, to cunnilingus, fellatio, or intercourse. The sexual behavior may occur only once but typically is repetitive for a period of three to four years before discovery or termination. The victims can be mere infants, but more often they are children of latency age or in their early teens. Usually, the victim is the eldest daughter living at home. When she leaves, the next youngest child often becomes involved. The victim may be taught in some cases, to become an active participant, eventually acting in a seductive manner with her parent or seducer.

The use of force is rarely necessary, although 15 percent of the fathers may threaten or resort to it. Alcohol is thought to be involved in over one-half of the cases of incest. The father may be drunk at the initial occurrence and use alcohol as an excuse for his behavior. The family may also blame the alcohol for the father's behavior, thereby denying his—and their—true responsibility. Intercourse occurs in about half the cases; fondling and oral genital sex in about 20 percent. Venereal disease or pregnancy occurs about 5 to 10 percent of the time and may be the event that precipitates discovery and the end of the affair.

In 1971, a retrospective study found that one-third of 1,800 college students experienced some form of sexual abuse as children. More recent literature suggests that 20 to 35 percent of white, middle-class women had a sexual encounter with an adult male when young; 4 to 12 percent with a relative. In 1955, the yearly rate of incest was thought to be 2 cases among 1,000,000 people. This number was far too low. Estimates have risen to 1,000 cases per 1,000,000 people, or over 200,000 cases per year in the United States. At least 10 percent of

127

cases of physical child abuse involve sexual abuse. Incest is still being under-reported. Probably 90 percent of the cases go undetected—especially in the middle- and upper-class population.

While such statistics illuminate the scope of the problem, they do not describe its complicated nature. Incest is as much a symptom as a cause of individual and familial dysfunction. It results from complex shifts in the family and from the nonempathic, self-centered narcissistic use of children by *both* father and mother. Incest is found not only in chaotic, disorganized families but also among people who function well in other spheres of their lives.

Incest involves an extreme sense of mutual dependence. Parents involved in incest need the family to stay together, since both mother and father rarely feel that they can exist on their own. All family members are likely to play a role in this setup; the mother frequently colludes in familial shifts and role distortions and relinquishes the central female role to her daughter, often with the fantasy that this will keep her husband around. At times, the father is the warmer parent while the mother is cold, distant, and depressed.

Incestuous fathers sometimes look to their daughters for the love they did not receive from their wives or their parents. And the daughters are given a special place in the family. They are told, in a sense, that it is their job to hold the family together. Disclosure or emancipation then becomes a betrayal of family harmony. The victims feel guilty if they stay or if they go. Consequently, suicidal behavior can accompany incest; it is used as a way out. Superficially, these families can appear quite normal, as in the following case. The distortion in familial structure is not always apparent to the casual observer.

The first time Linda spent the night with her father was when her mother was out of town. He said he was lonely and wanted her to join him. She was eleven years old. Although he did fondle her genitals, they did not have intercourse that evening.

Linda's father was principal of the regional high school. He was strict with Linda and her younger brother and sister. For instance, they had a long list of chores to do before they could spend time with their friends. On Saturday nights, when Linda was older, her father would quiz her about what she had done on dates, and he warned her repeatedly against promiscuity.

As Linda matured, her father became jealous when she went out with her friends or with boys. Sometimes he brought her flowers on the evening of a date. He gave her Valentine's Day cards and "courted" her in other ways.

As in many incestuous families, Linda experienced little privacy while growing up. Her father often walked into her room unannounced, even while she was dressing. If she was in the bathroom he would come in "just to talk." If the door was locked he still knocked and tried to get in.

They first had intercourse when her mother and brother were at a Cub Scouts meeting and the sister was asleep. Intercourse occurred regularly after that, mostly on weekends when the mother and brother were out. Sometimes when "tucking her into bed," Linda's father would fondle her. Usually he would also ask her to masturbate him.

Linda's mother seemed oblivious to what was going on. She was active in church work and other community activities and frequently was not at home. When Linda was fifteen her mother was hospitalized for a brief period because of alcoholism. During this time Linda assumed most of her mother's household duties. Even when her mother returned Linda was expected to continue this work.

Linda was terrified of telling anyone what was going on. At times, when he was gone, she would sit in her father's bedroom staring at his pistol or think about overdosing with his sleeping pills. When she graduated from high school she went away to college, against her father's wishes. There she had several affairs with older men and became pregnant by one of them, a friend of her father's. She had an abortion. Two years later she dropped out of school, married, and moved to another state. Shortly thereafter she was hospitalized following a serious suicide attempt. Linda's father had, by that time, begun an affair with his younger daughter.

In part, incest results from a maladaptive response to alterations in the husband-wife relationship. Incest can be triggered by a husband's dissatisfaction with his wife and more frequently, the wife's withdrawal from the family. These shifts make incest possible. Linda's mother was unavailable for a variety of reasons and the father then inappropriately turned to his daughter. The incestuous relationship was cemented by varying degrees of guilt, fear of retaliation, shame, and, possibly, unconscious gratification. Linda's later behavior also illustrated the promiscuity and intense feelings of guilt frequently experienced by victims of incest.

## THE MATRIX OF INCEST

A number of characteristics are usually found in families where incest is discovered. The daughter, even at an incredibly early age, becomes the central female in the household, taking over many of the maternal roles. The young child may cook, clean, iron, minister to, and sexually care for her father. The mother's abrogation of traditional maternal and wifely functions may be precipitated by a physical illness, leaving home for school or job, pregnancy (16 percent of cases occur during this time), or by various incompatibilities with her husband. Linda's mother was often away from home on business, and she also suffered from alcoholism. Such mothers abandon both their husbands and their children and are functionally absent from the home. One victim said: "My mother would come home and go right to bed. I was the mother for the night."

This abandonment is often more emotional than physical; the family's maladaptive response to the mother's desertion is to have the daughter assume the maternal role. Linda's mother was content to have Linda take care of her husband. The father, in turn, because of his own dependency needs, sense of low self-esteem, insecurity, and fears of humiliation, looks to his daughter to replace his lost wife. Thus, the inappropriate relationship between husband and daughter frequently has the mother's unconscious sanction; at times, she may actively promote it. Finally, because the family is so mutually dependent and because many of these people feel that they cannot function on their own, all deny the incest in order to keep the family together.

**The Father**

When found out, fathers often offer elaborate and bizarre rationalizations for their behavior. Some fathers say they want to "educate" their daughters at home so that they "do not have to be frightened of sex." Others state that they "didn't want to commit adultery." There are further ingenious excuses:

A Bible salesman, when asked why he began having sex with his eight-year-old daughter, said that he had glaucoma and had "mistaken" his daughter for his wife.

"My wife's gynecologist told us to abstain for one week because of fertility problems. I got very horny and had to have sex with my daughter . . . it was all the doctor's fault."

Other rationalizations that are sometimes heard include incest as a "folk cure" for venereal disease, as the answer to a "frigid" wife, or as the result of the daughter having "seduced" the father.

131

Obviously, the real reasons present a different picture. Some fathers, as might be expected, are sociopathic, indiscriminate, and dissolute; they lead chaotic lives. Alcohol may be involved, as well as the other violence syndromes such as suicide, child abuse, and spouse abuse. However, there is another group of fathers who appear outwardly stable and socially successful. These people, often religious, are solid citizens and the "pillars of their community." In fact, most incestuous fathers do not fit the stereotype of "child molesters," or "dirty old men." These fathers may be warm and giving parents, viewed by the community as nonaggressive, responsible men. Underneath it all, however, they are extremely dependent and fearful of rejection. They were also raised in uncertain environments and frequently experienced early deprivation or abandonment, overstimulation, and neglect. Many turn to their daughters for the care and love they did not get as children.

An example of such emotional neglect and overstimulation was described by an incestuous father who, as a child, slept in the same room as his parents until he left for college. At times his mother would get into bed with him. No overt sexual activity occurred but the seductiveness was obvious.

As their children get older, incestuous fathers show excessive interest in their daughter's personal activities. They express jealousy, restrict independence, and do not want them to be involved with other men. In general, they are frightened of losing their daughters and of reexperiencing the feelings of deprivation of their own childhood.

When emotional or physical access to the wife is somehow disrupted, this combination of unsatisfactory relationships with their wives, general insecurity, and uncertainty with women makes it likely that these fathers will look to the family, rather than outside, for companionship. Often these men do not have affairs with other adults because they are insecure with adult women. They are not homosexual but are frightened of being found sexually wanting. These fathers often court their daughters and treat them as true lovers. They use their parental influence to find safe, nonthreatening women who, unfortunately, are their children. The following cases illustrate the profound insecurities and strikingly low self-esteem characteristic of these men:

A father, himself a victim of child abuse and neglect, thought that the women he was interested in "were way above me—no way would they want me." Instead, he began a sexual relationship with his daughter that continued until she left for medical school.

A pilot said that he was always frightened of approaching strange women. He attempted a brief liaison with a stewardess but was impotent. He then settled on his eldest daughter, with whom he had sex until she ran away to another state. He then began having sex with his next oldest daughter.

## The Mother

Mothers involved in incest have often been victims of incest, abuse, or emotional neglect in childhood. As mothers, they may be absent from the home or otherwise dysfunctional. Twenty percent suffer from physical illnesses that precipitate those changes in family structure that are part of the picture of incest.

Mothers may consciously or unconsciously encourage the father-daughter affair, especially if the mother is sick or disabled or otherwise preoccupied. Certainly, incest cannot occur without their overt or covert participation. They are frightened of losing their husbands but also use their daughters as a buffer in the marital relationship:

A mother told an eight-year-old daughter to take her place in bed with her husband because she "wasn't feeling well" and wanted to sleep in the living room. She told her daughter that her father didn't like staying alone and liked having his back rubbed before going to sleep.

133

A woman who worked a paper route expected her twelve-year-old daughter to wake up her husband at 6:00 A.M., prepare his breakfast, and fix his lunch. Her eldest daughter, who lived out of the house, already had had sex with him and had warned the twelve-year-old about it. When the incest with the twelve-year-old was finally revealed, everyone "knew" about it except the mother.

Another mother frequently encouraged her husband to take their adolescent daughter shopping for clothes, even though she knew that the father insisted on fitting the daughter himself. He had been having an incestuous relationship with his daughter for over six years and had the daughter sleep with him while his wife was out of town.

Such wives rarely report incest and, when told about it, often accuse their children of lying. The extent of their denial is astonishing. They really cannot acknowledge what has been happening, even though it has occurred before their eyes. It is more important for these women to maintain an outward appearance of normality than expose themselves to the shame of disclosure. They are so dependent that they lie in order not to lose their husbands and their families. This sense of underlying dependent depression is found in most of these mothers. One victim said of her mother: "There were so many mirrors in the house—she must have been very lonely."

Predictably, incestuous mothers are emotionally neglectful of their children. They are self-involved, narcissistic, and immature; they may try to behave as their child's "best friend" and "confidante"—more like a sister than a parent. They do not respond to their children in age-appropriate, empathic ways but turn to their daughters too early for support, advice, and help with the family. They may also overtly compete with their daughters, comparing appearance and make-up, or they may denigrate their children's attempts at success and inde-pendence—a reflection, no doubt of their own upbringing.

## THE DISCLOSURE CRISIS

Public disclosure occurs in few cases. The majority of affairs end when the daughter gets pregnant, leaves home via an early marriage, runs away, or commits suicide. Some cases of incest may be revealed during family arguments, or the victim may tell her best friend, who then tells her own parents. Other cases are identified by the schools, or when the victim or parent lets a physician in on the secret. Interestingly, at the time of discovery many of the victims suffer from somatic complaints for which they had sought medical help.

The time of disclosure is a dangerous time for all. The parents will become even more depressed as the family threatens to break up. Suicide is a definite possibility, especially for the father, who, aside from possibly losing his family, may lose his social status in the community. Daughters also are at risk, especially if the parents blame them for the incest or the "betrayal." Even without overt accusation, children usually feel responsible. A young woman's unrealistic appraisal of her own actions may lead to self-mutilation, suicide, or other self-destructive behavior in a never-ending attempt to exculpate herself. If handled properly, the time of disclosure can be a time of therapeutic opportunity. This may be one of the few times that the family will be motivated to change. Much depends on how the news of the incest is handled by others. Response to the disclosure—how friends, family, social workers, police, physicians, lawyers, and judges behave—has a profound effect on how the victim and family will do in the long run. Public testimony, where the child is forced to disclose the most intimate details openly in court and to point the finger at her father, clearly is detrimental. On the positive side, the disclosure crisis represents an opportunity for the family to begin to deal with their long-standing problems. Their defenses are down and they are as ready as they ever will be to accept psychotherapeutic and social interventions.

## THE EFFECTS OF INCEST

What happens to children who are involved in incest? How wounded are they? This depends as much on how disturbed the family is and the emotional context of the incest as on the sexual activity itself. The child's relationship to the offender (the closer, the worse the effect), the age of the child when the abuse occurred, the presence of violence, and the general pattern of emotional abuse and exploitation all are important. If there is disclosure, the response of relatives, friends, and physicians also influences the long-term prognosis and eventual outcome for the victim.

*All* victims of incest feel responsible, in some way or another, for what happened. They misperceive themselves as the guilty ones; it is they who did something wrong—not their parents who betrayed them. Guilty ruminations are precipitated in part because these children were trained early to pay attention only to parental needs and to ignore their own. If they allow themselves to realize how deeply they were let down, they usually feel that they are being unjustly angry and critical toward their parents, which leads to further guilt. Trapped by their reactions to their parents' gross misbehavior, they continue to bear the burden of guilt while still trying to please. The guilt and distortions of reality can be extreme. One patient was convinced that it was her own fault that she was raped by one uncle and fondled by another when she was twelve. Her parents beat her when she told them about the attack. As an adult she continues to wonder whether she is too "sexual" in her interactions. For example, when a man opens a door for her, she feels that he can see that she is a "whore"—she does not see him as being friendly and polite.

Some children involved in incestuous relationships unconsciously feel chosen and special. Such feelings are another source of guilt and shame. The issue is of crucial importance in treatment, since these feelings are so unacceptable. It is apparent that some children receive gratification from distorted, exploitive relationships. They like being the central person in the family, so powerful that they can keep the family together. There may also be perverse sexual enjoyment. A twenty-eight-year-old woman said that sex with her father was "the best loving I ever had." In another case:

The middle of three daughters recalled that as a child she became very envious when her father did not choose her as the object of his affections when her oldest sister moved out of the house. The father chose his youngest daughter to continue the affair. The middle daughter felt depressed and humiliated that she, in some way, was not attractive enough for her father.

But it is important not to confuse what victims say with how they act. Some children involved in incest may on the surface appear to be unaffected, but most are withdrawn, some are seductive, and most are pseudomature. At a young age, victims may display a high incidence of behavioral disorders: bedwetting, nail biting, hyperactivity, and so forth. They exhibit symptoms of anxiety and depression. A history of incest is common in adolescent runaways, drug addicts, truants, juvenile delinquents, prostitutes, and adolescent suicides. Some victims may appear outwardly normal and well adjusted, be high achievers, and appear to be "perfect" children. But most will have difficulties with depression, intimacy, and anger stemming directly from the parental relationship. Often this becomes apparent as the victim moves into adulthood and parenthood.

Incest victims are raised in families where reality is distorted, and victims distort reality even further in order to ward off the intense feeling associated with the overstimulation of the incestuous relationship. Victims try to make the experience unreal or in other ways try to come to terms with what happened. One such adult patient reported that her life seemed to be made up of a series of discontinuous elements, that it was someone else who was incestuously involved with her father. Furthermore, she had no real idea of who she was and what she wanted out of life. Other victims resort to hypnoid, dissociative, or fugue states in order to split off, suppress, or deny the memories of the intense emotions associated with the incestuous relationship. Victims are unable to metabolize the trauma into their sense of who they are, and they experience altered states of consciousness when dealing with the incest, as in the case of a twenty-one-year-old woman who was brought to an emergency room because she was heard to scream, "daddy, daddy, daddy" during sleep. When she awoke she became mute and stared straight ahead. Her history revealed sexual involvement with her father and brothers. Having just married and left home, she had been overwhelmed with anxiety upon sexual contact with her husband and had reacted in the way described.

Many victims fail to develop a strong sense of self, self-worth, and autonomy. As children, they were forced to care for their parents sexually and in other ways. They develop independence prematurely and such independence is brittle and unreliable. They do not really have a solid sense of who they are; rather, they continue to take their cues primarily from the external environment. They have a hard time knowing what they feel. One victim of incest said: "I don't know who I am. I am just a reflection of other people's wishes." Another commented: "I don't think I exist. If someone drives, I'll just go along for the ride."

Attempts at reaching independence and developing autonomy may be experienced unconsciously as aggressive acts directed toward parents, since the parents made it clear that separation is betrayal of the family. Doing things for oneself is not allowed.

As adults, victims frequently engage in self-destructive behavior, repeatedly entering into unsatisfactory intimate relationships, unconsciously recreating the initial trauma while trying at the same time to master it and punish themselves. Victims may sexualize all their relationships, be promiscuous but also frigid, again acting out both sides of their ambivalence.

The following song lyrics illustrate many of these and other points. They were written by an adult victim:

Daddies, don't make your daughters grow up to
　be victims,
Don't let them know incest and childhood abuse,
Teach them a life that is based on the truth.

Daddies, don't make your daughters grow up to
　be victims,
Cause life is hard enough without that sort of
　stuff.
Just be the father they need.

A victim lives self-hate, destruction, and no sense
　of self-worth.
She thinks only of others, ignoring her needs all
　along.

She'll try to keep the peace even though it may mean
　a terrible internal self-war,
Though on the surface she'll act as if nothing is
　wrong.

Teach her about honesty, trusting, and liking her
　body.
Let her know that she is worthwhile and not just a
　slut off the street.
Never forget she is your daughter, adopted or
　natural,
Let her hold up her head and smile proudly at all
　she may meet.

Non-empathic parenting, exposure to abuse and over-stim-ulation, poor self-esteem, and an inability to function ade-quately in intimate relationships put incest victims at risk to repeat some form of abuse or neglect with their own children when they, in turn, become parents.

139

## THE INCEST TABOO

Recently, the incest taboo has been attacked as repressive, and the prohibition against incest has been compared to those previously existing for masturbation and homosexuality. Indeed, some people maintain that sexual activity between a parent and child may be beneficial; that the taboo inhibits familial warmth and affection. "Experts" have gone so far as to say that the taboo causes the difficulties experienced by participants in incest; they believe that without the taboo there would be no psychological morbidity attached to incestuous behavior.

This line of reasoning overlooks the pathogenic familial environments in which incestuous behavior occurs. It overlooks the fact that incest is symptomatic of underlying family problems, that incestuous parents exploit their children for their own emotional needs and do not allow them to develop in healthy, autonomous ways. Like any symptom, incest is a clue to an underlying pathogenic process. *It is incorrect to say that incest exists without concomitant serious familial pathology.*

The incest taboo is found in most cultures and the reasons for its existence are varied. Among animals the taboo is called the incest barrier, since it is thought to be biologically based. For humans, the taboo has biological, social, and cultural underpinnings.

Children of nonincestuous families are likely to be healthier and brighter and to have a longer life span than those who result from incestuous unions. For example, in one study of eighteen children who were products of incest, seven of the eighteen were normal at six months of age, three of the group were dead, and eight children were moderately to severely retarded. Therefore, the taboo probably has one of its origins in the biological advantages of avoiding inbreeding. There are social determinants as well. The taboo maintains order and provides a social structure in the family; roles are much more clearly defined in nonincestuous families. Such an

140

arrangement permits long-term dependence of children on their parents; the family can stay together even after the children reach sexual maturity. The taboo thus allows children to be trained and to absorb culture. It allows for the transmission of social values. Most importantly, the incest taboo allows love to be safe.

## COMMON REACTIONS TO INCEST

Incest is hardly a neutral subject. Nearly all people have to come to terms with their own incestuous wishes, fantasies, or experiences when faced with the reality of incest in others. Awareness of these responses makes it possible to be of greater use to the incest victim, family, or offender. Although the following reactions are normal, acting on them will usually just make matters worse.

1. *Feel outrage and extreme disgust.* Anger at the abusive nature of the incestuous relationship may be altruistically motivated, but it may also result from discomfort with one's own incestuous fantasies. People often condemn in others what they are ashamed of in themselves.

2. *Experience titillation and excitement.* Becoming stimulated by illicit sexual matters is a normal but usually disturbing response. Such titillation may provoke the observer to voyeuristic behavior such as prematurely or inappropriately seeking out the more intimate details of what happened. Some victims may by their learned seductive behavior, unconsciously induce this response. But this is another inappropriate use of the victim, this time by the observer.

3. Think that incest is perpetrated by *child molesters, crazy perverts, or dirty old men.* These labels distance the observer from the event and do not allow for an understanding of the family dynamics or individual difficulties that result in incest. Aside from being incorrect, these responses mean "they" do it, not "people like us." Calling incest a sin prohibits an empathic

141

stance. Calling the father a crazy pervert minimizes the complicated psychological problems in the father and severe maternal difficulties found in these cases.

4. Convince yourself that *incest occurs only in poor families.* This reaction is designed to make the incest "not me" once again. Incest may be more public among the disadvantaged and be more commonly part of a chaotic family picture. However, incest is frequently found in middle- and upper-class families. Because most potential casefinders in schools and hospitals are from these latter groups, their wishes to avoid finding incest close to home interfere with finding incest among the more privileged.

5. *Call the child a liar—the accusation of incest is false.* This is another attempt to make the trouble go away by pretending that incest did not happen. The number of parents who lie in these situations is far greater than the number of false accusations by children. Children past the age of three can be believed.

6. *Blame the daughter for seducing the father.* This rationalization deflects attention from parental responsibility and the distortion of familial roles. Certainly children can be very seductive. Some victims are more willing than others. Many daughters who are involved with incest *do* appear to be seductive and to sexualize their relationships. However, they were encouraged to behave this way by their adult seducers. Every little girl has a right to be seductive and to flirt with her father; it is a normal part of development. But no father has a right to take up his daughter's "offer."

7. *Agree that a little sex in the family doesn't hurt.* As mentioned, recently the incest taboo has been attacked as inhibiting a "warm" and "loving" atmosphere between parents and children; it has been said that frank sexual behavior between adults and children may even be beneficial. *In actual fact, the incest taboo probably allows parents and children to be emotionally even closer.* When everyone is certain of their limits, family members are more free to act within these constraints, since the boundaries are known in advance. A response of permissiveness also denies the seriousness of incest as an indication

of underlying family pathology: the exploitation of children by adults for their own needs.

## DANGER SIGNALS
## CLUES TO INCEST

Incest can be diagnosed and identified only if the possibility of its existence is admitted. Rarely are there physical signs of incest; there are few bruises or broken bones. With most children there will be *no* physical manifestations, since fondling, masturbation, and oral-genital contact leave no marks. Sometimes there is trauma to the genital area; thus, vaginal bleeding or other gynecological problems in a child or young adolescent can be clues to incest. However, the diagnosis of incest is usually made by observation of behavior and because of the history—not by physical findings. Only in the small percentage of cases where force is used will there be symptoms and signs of trauma.

The following are some of the more obvious danger signals. Many of these are symptoms of individual or family distress that, when discovered, must be investigated further.

• The *Perfect* family that always does everything together but includes a functionally absent mother. This mother may be depressed, ill, or in other ways emotionally unavailable, although she may be physically present. These families are often dominated by patriarchal and rigid fathers who are moral and righteous. These families are extremely close because they are terrified of losing one another.

• The *Chaotic* family, labeled as such by the community, which may participate in incest as one aspect of their general disorganization. The incest may be secret, but the other troubles are public, unlike the Perfect incest family, which seems superficially normal. Documentation of physical abuse or other chaotic life circumstances in a family must raise the question of concomitant sexual abuse.

• *Antisocial behavior.* Juvenile delinquency or other sociopathic behavior is often present in adolescent victims of incest. Prostitution, truancy, sexual promiscuity, stealing, and substance abuse are frequently found. Half of female runaways give sexual molestation as a reason for leaving home. Much of this behavior masks chronic depression, a sense of isolation, and low self-esteem. Workers in the field have labeled sexual promiscuity, runaway behavior, and suicidal activity the "incest triad."

• *General behavioral problems* in younger children. Enuresis, encopresis (eating feces), nightmares, behavioral disturbances, changes in appetite, and so forth are symptomatic of the anxiety and depression usually found in association with incest.

• *Role reversal.* Here the child assumes parental duties at an early age. At times the child seems "perfect" and very mature for her age. She does well at school, is very polite, and seems eager to please. For example, one victim of incest, besides getting straight A's in school, also began preparing most of her family's evening meals by the time she was ten. Another child never missed a day of school. There is a difference between a helpful, mature child and one who has been forced to take over the mother's role.

• Evidence of *over-stimulation* between the father and daughter with the functional or actual absence of the mother from home. Wrestling between father and adolescent daughter, bathing together, constant physical contact, and sleeping together may be clues to the presence of incest.

• Fathers *too interested in their daughter's personal life.* Incestuous fathers are intrusive about dates and other personal matters and do not allow their daughters enough privacy. Such problems result from the parent's inability to view his daughter as an independent person with a life of her own. These fathers will do anything to hold onto their daughters. Exhibitionistic strivings in parents may also be cause for alarm:

A thirty-six-year-old artist removed all the locks from the bathroom doors so that people could "come and go as they pleased." He slept in the nude and wouldn't dress when he walked around the home, even though his daughter was in her early teens and would have girl-friends over. He stated that nudity was "normal" and there was nothing to be ashamed of. Furthermore, he would walk into his daughter's room unannounced. When she returned from dates he would question her intently, asking for specific details about her sexual activity, and he would jealously complain that she seemed more interested in others than in himself.

These behaviors may be just passed off as eccentric or "modern." But they also can be symptomatic of incest.

• *Vague somatic symptoms.* Victims of incest suffer from head-aches, abdominal pains, or other somatic problems. They may make frequent visits to doctors or school nurses but not reveal the true state of affairs at home. Interestingly, parents in incestuous families have been described as suffering from multiple somatic problems as well. Probably this is due, in part, to the high incidence of anxiety and depression found among these people. Unfortunately, the vast majority of physicians misdiagnose these cases in both children and adults.

• *Perineal trauma.* Genital or oro-pharyngeal venereal dis-ease, vaginitis, urethritis, or other gynecological problems should raise the question of incest. *Pregnancy* in any young girl, but especially in a patient under twelve, is a strong indi-cation of sexual abuse.

## WHAT THEY SAY
## WHAT THEY MEAN

Denial or minimization of incest is likely to be the first response to any exploration of the subject. Where incest is suspected, the following are some of the common responses and what they really mean:

145

| Says | Means |
|---|---|
| What's wrong with a little affection between a father and a child? | I am very frightened that you will take my daughter away from me. Therefore, I can't tell you what is going on. |
| Nothing happened between me and my father. | I am terrified of betraying the family. If I confess then I will be getting my parents into serious trouble and I may lose my father. |
| Nothing happened between my husband and daughter, or She is lying | Although I know about the incest, I am frightened of losing my husband. I must protect my family at all costs—otherwise I'll be all alone. |
| It was a mistake. | I am very ashamed about what happened but I don't feel that I can tolerate a realistic self-appraisal of what is going on in my family. |
| It won't happen again. | It will. |

## GENERAL APPROACHES
## TO INCEST

The presence of incest may be discovered in different ways by a number of different people. Friends, co-workers, teachers, and physicians all have the chance to help these families. The problem is so widespread that there are many opportunities to come into contact with both victims and perpetrators.

## Commonly Made Errors

Once incest is suspected or discovered, there are a number of responses and maneuvers that will make matters worse. The following are some of the more detrimental approaches.

*Action:* Ignore the problem in the hope that the incest will stop.

*Result:* Incest is likely to cease only when there is a dramatic change in the family. The victim may marry early, run away, commit suicide, get pregnant, or otherwise leave the home. Most incestuous affairs, when discovered, have been in existence for at least three to four years. The disclosure crisis provides leverage to get family members into treatment— therefore, unless there is some active intervention, the affair is likely to continue.

*Action:* Talk to the parents but gratefully accept their denials and protestations.

*Result:* The majority of parents initially will deny any knowledge of incestuous activity, even when confronted directly. The victim, because of shame or fear of retaliation, will also minimize what has occurred, if she admits anything at all. Fears that the family will disintegrate if the truth becomes known keeps all family members silent. It is rare for the full extent of the incest to become apparent on initial inquiry.

*Action:* Arrange to send the daughter to a boarding school.

*Result:* "Getting rid" of the problem by exiling the daughter will do a number of things, none of them good. It will reinforce the notion that the daughter is the guilty party and should be ashamed of what she did; allow the father to take up with a younger sister—which will happen in about a third of the cases; allow the family to deny its own contribution to the present difficulties; and destroy an opportunity to get

147

people into treatment so that these pathological roles can be changed.

*Action:* Threaten the father with the police.
*Result:* Threats will serve only to isolate the father by creating more guilt and shame. The fear of disclosure is full of danger—as well as opportunity for change. Fathers will become extremely anxious and depressed, and suicide may be precipitated by such threats. In fact, suicide is a possibility for all the participants when the incest is disclosed.

*Action:* Tell the father that he should see a psychiatrist, since he must be crazy for being sexually involved with his daughter.
*Result:* The offender should receive psychiatric care, but not as a punishment. This maneuver focuses the blame only on the perpetrator and obscures the fact that the problem involves the entire family. Without the wife's participation, treatment of the father will fail to address the whole family's problem. The wife's collusion and active promotion of the incestuous affair must be examined. In addition, most victims of incest will need psychiatric care to help deal with their guilt, low self-esteem, and depression.

*Action:* Gossip with others about the possibility of incest.
*Result:* Incestuous families typically are extremely intradependent, rarely looking outside the family unit for support. They find it difficult to expect help, since their ability to trust has been stunted by childhood experiences. Vulnerable to criticism, these people quickly sense disapprobation. With their fears of rejection confirmed, they will withdraw from social interaction and increase their pathological dependency on one another, thereby making it even less likely that they will tolerate changes in their relationships.

148

## Helpful Interventions

The following are some guidelines and approaches that may be taken when dealing with incest. Other possibilities may suggest themselves.

Be as nonjudgmental as possible. Do not criticize the father to the victim, since the child still loves the parent. It is always important to *support the rightness of disclosure,* as it will be accompanied by the victim's guilt and shame. Remember that children may explain things in nonadult ways; role play with dolls or other playthings may give a true picture of what has happened. Finally, it is important throughout any evaluation to reaffirm to the child that the *incest was not the fault of the child.*

The crisis of disclosure will cause severe stress in the family; support, kindness, and understanding from other family members and friends is critical for a successful outcome whether or not the family stays together. Since all participants suffer from extreme guilt and low self-esteem, continued outside acceptance from others will be of great help.

The following questions have been utilized to explore the presence of incest. These should be helpful to family, friends, and physicians and can be asked of the child or any family member:

• What are the sleeping arrangements at home? Who shares which bedrooms? Are there locks on the bedroom doors? Is privacy respected?

• What are the bathing arrangements? Do people bathe together, and at what age are they separated? What is the family attitude toward nudity in the home?

• Has there ever been concern about too much physical affection between a parent and a child? Are there things going on in the home that people are too embarrassed or ashamed to talk about? Has there ever been sexual contact between a parent and a child?

The quality of the parental relationship will be explored by the following: How recently have the parents gone out alone? How is their sexual relationship? Were they sexually abused as children? Has the mother been absent from the home? Is she ill? Does either parent have trouble with alcohol?

It may be useful to speak in private with the family member most familiar to you and express your concerns. Explain that you intend to call a child protection service but that you hope the family will seek psychological help on their own. This intervention should not replace filing a report, since denial is the usual response from most family members. Not reporting will lead to greater danger for the family and the victim. The worry that the family will "get into trouble" is usually a rationalization; they are in a tremendous amount of trouble already.

The following applies to friends, families, and clinicians: when you contact a child protection service, be specific in the report. Neither minimize nor exaggerate what is known. Outline your concerns and what evidence you have. States have reporting laws mandating that certain professionals make their suspicions known. They also provide for anonymity of the reporter.

Be persistent until you are satisfied that the case has received proper attention. Although the suspicion of incest may prove to be unfounded, this can only be judged by trained professionals.

Outside agencies also provide the necessary structure and support to help families reestablish proper relationships and reduce the effect of guilt and shame on the participants. At the very least, the child will be protected. In fact, *legal involvement is the only way many such families will enter treatment and stay long enough for meaningful change to occur.*

## THE MEDICAL EVALUATION
## OF INCEST

The diagnosis of incest rests primarily on the history; the medical evaluation seeks to corroborate the story. Since incestuous behavior can range from sexual fondling to, infrequently, violent genital penetration, physical findings will be inconsistent and not always helpful in making the diagnosis. Therefore, the lack of physical evidence does not disprove the existence of incest.

Physicians will encounter victims *and* perpetrators of incest in a number of different situations. Both parents and children may show symptoms and signs of stress and make vague somatic complaints, and there will be findings more directly related to incest. However, physician discomfort and a low index of suspicion usually contribute to few cases being identified.

## Commonly Made Medical Errors

*Action:* Do not fully evaluate patients with multiple somatic complaints—for example, headaches, back pain—for the danger syndromes.

*Result:* Incest continues and cases are missed. Patients under stress complain of vague somatic distress in a covert plea for help that is usually unconscious. The physician should get beyond these symptoms in order to delineate the nature of the stress. Evaluating the potential for abuse, incest, and suicide is part of this examination. For example, a forty-seven-year-old woman came to the emergency room complaining of headaches. She seemed anxious and depressed and mentioned that her adolescent daughter had just moved to the basement and put a lock on her door. She repeated this a number of times. The woman then waited patiently until the doctor specifically asked if her husband was attempting to have sexual relations with her daughter. The answer was yes.

*Action:* When incest with one child is uncovered, fail to evaluate the other children that live in the home.

*Result:* Cases of multiple incest are not uncommon and will be overlooked if the other children are not evaluated. In chaotic families, it is not unusual to find several forms of abuse between parent and child, including the coexistence of homosexual and heterosexual abuse. Suicide is a definite possibility in such situations, as are problems with alcohol and other behavioral disturbances.

*Action:* Neglect to report the case to child protection services because the victim no longer lives at home.

*Result:* The father may seduce his next youngest daughter or the children of other families, since once the original victim is out of the home fathers may turn elsewhere. Although most perpetrators will not molest other children, some do make sexual advances to their daughter's friends or other children.

## Helpful Medical Interventions

The evaluation of incest should take place in an unhurried manner in a quiet room conducive to relaxation. The child may interpret a medical evaluation as yet another assault from an adult. Therefore, tact is necessary. Questions should be followed by enough time to let the patient take the conversation where she wants to. Watch for hesitancy, embarrassment, denial, or other signs of discomfort. To avoid misdiagnosis, it is important to gather information from as many sources as possible, such as other agencies, the medical chart, and, possibly, family members.

Sexual abuse is often not revealed during one visit to a physician. It may be uncovered over a series of visits as the patient (parent or child) becomes more comfortable with the clinician and as the clinical picture becomes more clear. Physicians can be very explicit in their questioning and patients will not feel too uncomfortable if the interview is handled properly. The areas of inquiry outlined on pages 149–50 should be followed in any situation where incest is suspected. In addition, particularly useful are such questions as: "Are there things going on at home about which you are uncomfortable or too ashamed to talk about?" "Has there been any sexual contact between family members in your home besides between your parents?" and so forth.

Inhibitions tend to emanate from the doctor, not the patient. If the presence of incest is almost certain, the following medical approaches should be taken:

Were foreign objects used? Did the victim do anything after the sexual contact that would affect the presence of specimens, such as douching or brushing teeth? A thorough contraceptive and menstrual history should also be obtained.

Precision during history taking is extremely important. Specific questions should be posed: What are the number of contacts? When, where and with whom did they occur? *Remember that more than one adult may be sexually abusing a child.* For example, a father and an older brother may be sexually active with a daughter.

The patient should be evaluated for trauma, bruising, and other signs of physical assault, and a detailed description should be placed in the chart. If a pelvic examination is necessary, it should be performed by someone expert in examining children. Occasionally it will have to be done under anesthesia. The following should be looked for:

- genital injuries and anal tears
- vaginal tears
- injuries to the penis in male victims
- trauma to the perineum
- other signs of bodily injuries
- signs of venereal disease: chancres or ulcers in the mouth, vagina, or rectum.

Laboratory tests should also be obtained: genital, anal, and throat cultures for gonorrhea; blood tests for syphilis, with another exam in six weeks; pregnancy tests; and forensic specimens such as semen, pubic hair combings, and nail scrapings. The child's clothing should be saved and the chain of evidence followed carefully so that specimens can be adequately identified in court. People will be required to testify what safeguards were followed with all specimens obtained. Therefore, emergency rooms should have protocols for these matters.

A follow-up visit for the patient should be made to examine for the later development of signs of venereal disease or pregnancy.

Finally, even if no physical evidence of incest is present, but it is still suspected, the physician is required to report his or her suspicions. People involved in incest should also be referred for a psychiatric evaluation. This should be done on an emergency basis if the danger of lethal behavior is judged to be high.

## EMERGENCY PSYCHIATRIC INTERVENTIONS

The psychiatric evaluation may take place in conjunction with the medical examination. The goals of emergency psychiatric treatment are to protect the child from further sexual abuse and to encourage the family to begin to rely on less pathological modes of interaction. It must be remembered that *all* the people in such families, particularly the victim, will be difficult to engage in treatment because they feel that they do not deserve to do well and will be betraying the family if they change their behavior.

### Commonly Made Psychiatric Errors

The following are some common mistakes made during the emergency evaluation of incest. Although not irreversible, they do increase the risk of further psychological morbidity and mortality.

*Action:* Raise the question of incest but leave the family to its own devices without providing adequate follow-up, treatment, and support.

*Result:* Such an approach may lead to destabilization of incestuous families and thus to overwhelming emotion and chaos. The time of disclosure is most dangerous. These families are not mutually supportive and family members may resort to precipitous action in order to deal with the accusations of incest. Further maladaptive responses may be resorted to, such as an increase in violence, use of alcohol, suicide attempts, and spouse abuse.

*Action:* Despite signs of mounting anxiety and panic, ask the victim to be explicit about what occurred.

*Result:* Victims of incest often have difficulty tolerating intense feelings and try to keep such feelings or memories of the actual events out of consciousness. To challenge this defense before an adequate therapeutic alliance exists, risks flooding the patient with emotion she is not yet ready to handle. She may become mute, overwhelmed with anxiety, or suicidal. Asking exactly *what* happened may be demanding that the patient remember events she is not ready to remember. Specifics can be asked for, but only at the right time. This should be done empathically and not in an intrusive way.

*Action:* Treat the family as a unit and fail to see them individually.

*Result:* Treatment of the family with all members present will allow the parents to gang up on the child before the parents fully accept their own contribution to the incest, thus increasing the victim's guilt and causing the treatment to fail. Parents are often more concerned about proving their own innocence than helping their child. Victims, at least initially, need to be seen separately in order to work with their intense guilt and poor self-esteem and to protect them from parental attacks.

*Action:* Tell the victim that she is exaggerating.

*Result:* Children involved in incest rarely embellish the facts—usually they play them down. However, they often are willing to accept the blame for the abuse and such an accusation may precipitate a suicide attempt. It cannot be stressed enough that victims need to be told that what happened is not their fault. Victims ALWAYS feel guilty—no matter what the circumstances. This has to be taken into consideration before therapeutic intervention can be successful.

*Action:* Tell the victim that she "enjoyed" the incest and her special place in the family.

*Result:* This intervention is premature, inappropriate, and possibly incorrect. Certainly, the timing is all off—such things may be discussed after some time in treatment, if they are discussed at all. Such interpretations run the risk of flooding the victim with anxiety and guilt, which she then may deal with by resorting to suicide or other self-destructive behaviors.

*Action:* Assume the major problems are dealt with once the family is separated and the incest has ceased.

*Result:* After disclosure and cessation of the incest, many problems still remain. The child will be blamed for "causing" problems for the family; fathers may feel guilty, ashamed, and abandoned; and mothers will feel ineffectual and confused. Treatment of long-standing problems in the parents and children may take years. Suppressing the symptom does not arrest the disease. The pathological underpinnings of the incest must be examined and brought to light in order to minimize the chances for further episodes. Other associated difficulties—such as alcoholism, the various forms of physical abuse, depression, suicide, and so forth—must also be evaluated. Victims of incest may require psychotherapeutic help long after the sexual activity has ceased.

## Helpful Emergency Interventions

Overcoming the family's denial, after it is determined that the child is safe, is the cornerstone of emergency psychiatric treatment. The admission of a problem and at least three people's involvement in it (mother, father, and daughter) is crucial to a successful therapeutic outcome. But if the family's denial is maintained, particularly by the parents, then the prognosis is especially poor. Family members must have some wish to change if treatment is to be successful: the mother must reestablish her maternal role and the father has to stop turning to his daughter to fulfill wifely functions. These maladaptive maneuvers have to cease in order for the family to remain together. With many of these families, court-ordered treatment is especially helpful to overcome the initial phase of denial.

Removal of the father from the home is not always necessary to allow the daughter to remain, especially if adequate supervision is available and the mother acknowledges the problem. At times, emergency foster home placement for all children may be necessary, especially if the mother is unreliable. This may give people time to gather their wits, overcome the shock of exposure, perhaps avoid recriminations, and allow for longer-term plans to be worked out. Often children are inappropriately placed in foster care; it is the father who should be removed from the home. Patients should be in constant contact with case workers or therapists and threatened decompensations should be identified early. Hospitalization may be necessary for the victim or perpetrator if the danger of suicide, homicide, or regression is high.

Obtaining information about exactly what happened is crucial but can be anxiety-provoking for both therapist and patient. However, this information is critical and if done properly can help relieve the patient of feelings of loneliness and guilt when the clinician eschews criticism. The following dialogue is an example of how specific the questioning should be and how uncomfortable it is. This is a conversation with the father of an eight-year-old girl:

Q: Tell me what happened with your daughter.
A: We just kissed.
Q: Anything else?
A: Once she touched my zipper.
Q: Only once? What else did she do?

157

A: Well—she pulled my zipper down and put her hand in—that was all. [Pause] She did it more than once.
Q: Did you do anything besides let her touch you?
A: Well [pause], I put my finger in her vagina.
Q: Anything else? Did you try to enter her?
A: No, I only had her blow me and I put my finger in.

The examiner must, of course, be sensitive to the possibility of mounting panic or anxiety and be prepared to back off from the history taking.

Long-term treatment and change are possible, but the degree of change will be determined, in part, by the family's reaction to the initial phases of the evaluation. If this goes well, the prognosis is better; if the family is abused by inept professionals, and maintain their denial, then the outlook is dim.

An adequate longitudinal history should be obtained that includes the following:

• the quality of the parental relationship
• the distortion of family roles; for example, who takes care of whom?
• the specific function of the daughter in the family
• childhood histories of the parents, looking especially for incest, child abuse, or other types of parental deprivation
• what factors triggered the incestuous behavior
• the present danger of other self-destructive behaviors

These factors were illustrated by a high-school teacher who said that he began masturbating with his seven-year-old daughter when his wife started an affair with a colleague. He felt at a loss, humiliated and helpless. Although he was not raised in an abusive family, both of his parents died when he was a small child and he always felt as if he were a "guest" no matter where he lived. He felt that his daughter was the only person he could rely on and who would not desert him. But because of overwhelming guilt he entered treatment voluntarily.

158

Psychotherapy that focused on his poor self-esteem, fears of loneliness, and problems with intimacy reduced the risk of incest and allowed this patient to function more adequately as an adult, and the marriage remained intact. His daughter also entered psychotherapy where she, too, did well.

Treatment can be complicated by the fact that some therapists are unable to tolerate the notion that incest has indeed occurred at all. The therapists blame it on the patient's unconscious and make incest unreal at the same time, as in the following:

A college student confessed to her psychiatrist that she had sexual relations with her father, a noted marine biologist. She had difficulty remembering the details, since things went "blank and discontinuous" in her mind when she thought about it. Furthermore, she feared that she had "made the whole thing up." The psychiatrist said that it "didn't matter" what the true facts were since she had the wish to seduce her father anyway.

This destructive intervention heightened the victim's sense of guilt, ignored the abrogation of parental responsibility, blurred the distinction between wishes and reality, and further weakened the patient's grasp of events. During a later treatment the patient was supported in her attempts in distinguishing reality from fantasy; she was assured that her father was, in fact, wrong. Yet this took a long time for her to believe, especially in light of her earlier treatment.

Finally, it should be said again that the victim be supported in her disclosure and told that she is not responsible for what happened. However, clinicians must be careful not to take sides, since all the participants in incest are in need of psychotherapeutic help for their underlying depressions and inability to function autonomously.

# 5

# Spouse Abuse

Train a child in the way he should go: and
when he is old, he will not depart from it.

*Proverbs 22:6*

Spouse abuse is, for most, child abuse and neglect grown
up; simply a new edition of an old story. It is not coincidence
or bad luck when a man or woman becomes involved with,
and remains in, an abusive situation. Adult abuse, because of
its kinship to child abuse, is a widespread occurrence in all
social classes and involves problems of poor self-esteem and
extreme dependence in *both* the perpetrator and victim. Weak,
ineffectual, dependent, and depressed spouses beat their
mates; weak, ineffectual, dependent, and depressed mates
remain in such relationships. *Both* were usually abused when
young. For men, the macho image is a cover for fears of failure, loss, or humiliation. Aside from physical violence, spouse
abuse also encompasses a wide range of behaviors that includes
emotional abuse and denigration. All types of abuse are usually minimized and overlooked, frequently with dangerous
results for both participants as well as the children who are
exposed to parental indifference, violence, and mutual neglect.

160

Children of such families are at risk, for they are likely to grow into abusive or victimized adults.

Spousal abuse represents the systematic brutalization, verbally or otherwise, of someone who feels, or is, helpless to effect a change of circumstances by someone who feels the same way. The severity of the beatings is often less important than the emotional context in which they occur, why they occur, and whether there is opportunity to change this maladaptive mode of interaction.

Some form of physical violence is said to occur in half of American families. And violence between intimates is usually more brutal than between strangers. In any one year, close to two million people use or threaten to use a knife or gun on their mates. Many more assault each other verbally, threaten, or use other types of force. The true magnitude of spousal violence is not really known, partly because of under-reporting, and partly because of confusing terminology in this area. What constitutes one couple's violence can be another's "normal" behavior. Screaming, for example, can be perceived as truly violent; verbal threats can be as emotionally harmful as physical abuse.

Although the predisposition to violence is ubiquitous, not everyone loses control and acts. Various factors make violence more likely. Anything that decreases impulse control, such as alcohol, raises the potential for violence. In addition, violence-prone individuals are unusually sensitive to certain sources of stress, which may appear minor to an outsider. These usually involve humiliation and loss, perceived or real. The potential aggressor feels helpless, impotent, and shamed, and thus compelled to act. Violence is a maladaptive way to right perceived wrongs, a way to hold onto, and not lose, an object from which love is yearned. Violence, then, is the result of diverse factors impinging on the individual; the greater the loading for violence, the greater the danger of abuse.

At one time or another, the possibility of participation in violence can be part of everyone's life. For most, if the stress is severe, some form of maladaptive behavior is the likely result. People become involved in mutually destructive behavior gradually. Without realizing when the line of abuse is crossed, couples become mutually destructive. The following case illustrates this drift into abuse. These people did not experience any overt violence in their marriage until they became prospective parents:

Susan was two months pregnant with their first child when Sam pushed her to the ground during an argument. Nothing happened until a week later when Susan wondered out loud if they could financially afford to have a child, since Sam's law practice was "so slow." She also complained that Sam was rarely home—he was spending too much time playing basketball. Sam left the house and returned later while Susan was taking a bath.

He wanted to join Susan in the bathtub but she refused, saying that she was too upset about their earlier conversation. "Besides," she said, "you already proved that you can get me pregnant."

The next argument, a week later, resulted in Sam pushing Susan out of bed and around the room. He hit her with little provocation. She told friends that her bruise was the result of falling over the piano stool on the way to the bathroom. She told her obstetrician the same thing on her next prenatal visit.

Susan experienced trouble sleeping and an increase in headaches. Sam spent most of his free time playing ball with his friends. He also got two traffic tickets, one for speeding and the other for running a red light. He also began drinking more.

At the end of the third month of the pregnancy Sam punched Susan in the eye during one of their interminable nighttime arguments. She then told her doctor what happened. This took courage because Susan was embarrassed and ashamed about what had occurred. However, the doctor explained that expectant fathers often were under stress and not to worry, that Sam was a sensible person and things "would work out."

A week later Susan aborted when she was pushed down the basement stairs. This followed her demand that Sam spend less time out of the house and more time with her. During the fight, Susan threw a vase at Sam and then tried to get out of the way. He caught up to her and punched her in the back. When she ran for the basement, he pushed her down the stairs.

Later it was learned that both Sam and Susan were raised by cold, aloof parents. Sam remembered being publicly humiliated by his father for "only getting B's." At other times his father would lose control while punishing him and once gave him a black eye. Sam said that although he felt close to his mother, he wondered why she did not protect him more. These dormant issues were reactivated by the stress of pregnancy. Previous memories of maladaptive patterns emerged under pressure.

The risk of spousal violence rises during periods of family turmoil and change. Pregnancy is such a high-risk time. Weak fathers feel threatened by the prospective rival for their wife's attention; they are fearful of being replaced. Sam probably thought that he was losing his dominant place in Susan's life. Although provoked, his responses indicated an underlying sense of helplessness and inferiority. His violence was a maladaptive response to difficult times. Another father echoed his competition with his child by becoming enraged at his wife's attentive behavior toward their son on the boy's first birthday. He said, "She ignores me now, somehow I feel less important than him."

The functional "loss" of the wife to the child becomes intolerable to dependent, ineffectual men. It is not unusual for extramarital affairs, increased alcohol consumption, or other signs of distress to accompany the coming of fatherhood. For example, one-sixth of all cases of father-daughter incest are

163

initiated when the mother is functionally "absent" during pregnancy. In addition, because of the increased risk of family violence during the prepartum period, abused mothers experience a higher incidence of miscarriages and abortions than others. Therefore, unusual problems during pregnancy should raise the suspicion of spousal violence. Unfortunately, Susan's physician did not appreciate the danger.

Spouse abuse is not "supposed" to be a middle-class phenomenon. However, spousal violence occurs in all segments of society, though it may be that less privileged groups resort to *physical* violence more readily. It is also true that violence is more "public" in these groups; these people are more likely to appear on police blotters and in city hospital emergency rooms than in private physician's offices. Because of same-class bias, middle-class professionals minimize middle-class abuse.

## THE REPETITION OF ABUSE
## THE CYCLE OF VIOLENCE

No single explanation sufficiently tells *why* couples abuse each other *when* they do it. In fact, many explanations in this area are often illusory—they explain very little. As a generalization, however, it is safe to say that *violence begets violence; that many of those involved in adult abusive situations were exposed to violence and neglect as children.* Poor early relationships make the child less well-equipped to deal with the exigencies of later life. At times of stress, these people are more likely to resort to violence. They also view violence as an acceptable option.

Later factors, such as cultural attitudes, "learning" violence, or particular social circumstances influence the generation of violence but not with the same primacy as do earlier relationships. Alcoholism, the decline of the extended family, overcrowding, social customs, and financial circumstances are all important. But parental deprivation and childhood abuse and neglect are consistently found in the histories of people who resort to adult abuse and neglect. And the childhood abuse and neglect is not always obvious—subtle denigration or cold and aloof parents often will be enough to increase the likelihood of adult violence.

Participants in spousal violence experience shame and guilt over being repetitively involved in abusive situations. Many victims of abuse feel that they caused their own troubles. Abused children wonder what they did wrong, and when they become adults, they feel the same way. Some abused people fail to label the abuse; they say, "I deserved every beating that I got." This has important implications for treatment, since these people confuse love and intimacy, violence and brutality. Often, when one abusive relationship ends, another is begun, either as perpetrator or victim. These people endlessly repeat destructive patterns learned at an early age. The following example of repetitive, hard-core abuse is extreme; other cases are more subtle but the cycle of violence, its antecedents and repetitive nature, cannot be missed:

Jojo, a twenty-eight-year-old woman, came to her physician complaining of a vaginal discharge. He noted multiple bruises on her arms, chest, abdomen, and legs and obtained a history of spousal violence. She told the following story of constant involvement in maltreatment:

Her current boyfriend had severely beaten her twenty-two times. Two months before, he broke her nose—for the third time. She admitted that she was concerned about her health but was afraid of losing him. "I'd rather have someone who loves me ten days out of the month than no one loving me at all."

She said she had been her father's favorite, the youngest of his three children. He, however, deserted the family when she was six and she never saw him again.

As long as she could remember, her mother told JoJo that she was a "bad, disgusting person just like your father." She remembered her mother repeating "I hate

165

you" throughout the years. When she was sexually molested by her mother's boyfriend, at age seven, her mother blamed her for this, calling her a "slut" and a "whore." Once her mother tried to strangle JoJo during an argument and another time tried to suffocate her with a pillow. Both times the patient got away with "only" minor bruises.

Because of numerous beatings, the patient ran away frequently during her teen-age years. She escaped home when she married a boy she recently met who, too, beat her regularly and was unfaithful. She bought him a Corvette in order to "keep him," but he deserted her for another woman.

JoJo, who had two children by this time, met a "very nice man," with whom she began living. She did not find him "very romantic or exciting." She left him for her current boyfriend.

Soon after she met this man he began beating her. She said that the most recent violence occurred when she asked him whether he loved her; he had been spending much of his time away from home. She wondered what she was "doing wrong" and why she couldn't be a "better" girlfriend.

This woman's self-concept, like that of most people involved in abuse, was extremely poor. She believed what she learned early in life: that to be loved was to be beaten and abused; that she deserved to suffer. The only person who really "loved" JoJo, her father, had deserted her as a child. Consequently, she repeatedly engaged in self-destructive relationships in order to recreate earlier relationships and to punish herself for being so bad. Fortunately, not all victims of violence are as self-destructive as JoJo. Not all cases are this obvious, but the issues are usually the same. The old vaudeville joke has applicability here:

Q:  When did you realize he stopped loving you?
A:  When he stopped beating me.

Repetitive involvement in destructive behavior also occurs in the service of mastering past traumas; the victim becomes the aggressor—becomes, in a sense, the parent. In this way, old fears of helplessness and vulnerability are confronted by making others feel hurt and helpless. It must be realized that these dynamics of recapturing and revenge can also be operative without the existence of physical violence. Emotional denigration, neglect, and verbal abuse are often sufficient ammunition. Actual physical violence may be present intermittently or altogether absent.

The repetitive nature of these difficulties is striking. Problems are frequently found in generation after generation, as JoJo and the following case illustrate:

In spite of the fact that a twenty-eight-year-old woman had to retreat to safe houses eight times in the two years she was married, she always called her husband to pick her up and take her home. He would usually begin abusing her in the car. He was an alcoholic railroad man "just like my father." Her father still severely abused her mother.

When concern was expressed about the fact that her husband was buying a gun she said proudly, "Don't men have a right to have guns?" She had little sense that things should, or could, be otherwise.

Thus, those involved in abuse see themselves as weak, ineffectual, dependent people with little ability to change their life or circumstances. They are unconsciously frightened of being deserted, which is why many remain in such relationships. Violence may not always be present but the nonempathic, demanding, and dependent way of relating usually is. A businessman, whose father used to beat him and lock him in a closet at the slightest transgression, was unable to maintain intimate relationships with women. He had repeated thoughts of humiliating and debasing them. Furthermore, he became easily enraged and verbally abusive toward them when he felt devalued.

167

Interestingly enough, the only women this man became involved with were those who had experienced some form of early parental deprivation. One was an adopted child, another lost a parent early in life, and another's mother was schizophrenic.

## POLYSYMPTOMATIC FAMILIES

Men, women, and families involved in spousal violence can also be involved with a number of other destructive behaviors. Both victim and perpetrator may be suicidal, before, during, or after the abuse. The danger that the perpetrator will commit suicide is especially high if the victim finally decides to make some changes and leave. Furthermore, after making homicidal threats, a person is more likely to kill himself than to kill someone else. If a homicide actually occurs, a significant number of spouse slayers will commit suicide before adjudication. Victims of spousal violence may also try to end violent relationships by attempting to kill themselves.

A twenty-eight-year-old machinist came to an emergency room following an overdose. The physician noted testicular swelling. The patient admitted to being kicked by his wife after an argument about her infidelity. His father, hearing of this, called him a "pussy" and "not much of a man." The patient took a near fatal overdose following this confrontation with his father.

At times spousal violence will coexist with child abuse and alcohol abuse, as in this case of a seventeen-year-old girl who came to the emergency room with two black eyes and a fractured cheekbone:

She had been beaten by both parents after returning home late from a date. The patient didn't seem overly concerned about the beating. She wondered, instead,

what she "did wrong" and hoped to be "better next time."
When she was younger her parents abused each other
regularly. However, once the daughter reached adolescence, they turned their attention to her. All three members of the family drank excessive amounts of alcohol.

This patient felt that she deserved to be beaten and most likely
would seek relationships throughout her life that would fulfill
this need.

The possibility of incest was raised in the following case of
spousal violence and child abuse:

A forty-eight-year-old man was brought to the emergency room by his ten-year-old son. He had a broken
arm inflicted by his wife who hit him with a hammer.
The son was frightened that his parents were going to
kill each other. He also said that his mother sometimes
beat him, too, often to the point where he left the house
and hid in the woods.

The patient said that his wife had hit him in the past,
with a hammer, but had never broken a bone. He
expressed severe embarrassment and said, "This doesn't
make me feel like much of a man in front of my son. He
worried that his son would grow up "feminine," since he
was still sleeping with his mother. The husband slept in
the basement.

## SPOUSE ABUSE AND MURDER

People usually kill people they know. Twenty to fifty percent of all murders in this country take place in the home; up
to forty percent between spouses. About an equal number of
wives kill their husbands as husbands their wives. However,
more women than men are seen as justified in their homicidal
behavior because of severe provocation by their husbands.
Wives tend to stab their husbands, while husbands choose any

method available, such as shooting, stabbing, and beating. Familiarity clearly breeds contempt, since murders within a family are much more violent than murders between strangers. Instances of multiple stabbings, shootings, burnings, and beatings are found in a very high proportion of murders between spouses.

More murders occur during the night, on weekends, and on holidays than at any other time. These are the times when family members are together. Forty percent of familial murders occur in the home and twenty percent in the bedroom, which is the place of greatest intimacy, highest vulnerability, and violence.

Some victims precipitate their own death. Therefore, the issue of who did what and to whom is not always clear. Twenty to forty percent of homicide victims are the first to use force or show a weapon during a confrontation. Seventy percent of these victims were found to be drinking at the time of death, as opposed to forty percent in nonvictim-precipitated murder. Another indication of the self-destructive potential of some victims is their fairly common history of past suicidal behavior.

## THE ROLE OF THE VICTIM

Spouse abuse is sometimes referred to as "wife battering," but this narrowing of the term underestimates the complicated nature of spousal violence. This ignores the fact that men are verbally abused and some beaten, and that some women do provoke attacks.

To some researchers, the concept of any victim-precipitated situation is anathema. In their view, female victimization can be explained primarily in terms of power relationships; women are conditioned to be victims and learn to be helpless at an early age, and they are helpless to change in the face of man's superior size and strength. Such a view minimizes the frequent participation of the victim and fails to note that men are often abused as well.

Some research suggests that men and women initiate violent acts in almost equal proportion. But women usually are more severely beaten because of men's superior size and strength. One kind of spousal violence, the "Saturday night" syndrome, is clearly characterized by mutual provocation. Men and women, usually while drunk, seek to slug it out with each other. Such relationships can go on for years.

The victim-perpetrator dichotomy is an oversimplification, not only because the victim may be the provocateur but because of other unconscious determinants to beat and be beaten. Sadism and masochism are factors that help explain why people remain in such relationships. Those who argue against this notion feel that it excuses the perpetrator and blames the victim. Nothing is farther from the truth, although the concept of masochism may be used defensively in this fashion. If we deny the complexity of abuse, it becomes more difficult to identify, to treat, and therefore to end.

Some form of attenuated abuse, the wish to hurt or be hurt, is part of most people's lives at one time or another. Fortunately, many men and women perceive any sort of physical abuse as outside the realm of acceptable behavior—if it occurs they will not tolerate it for long. Either the abuse ceases or the relationship is ended. These people's sense of self-worth protects them from further participation. However, other people seem actively to seek out violent situations and find a good "fit" with a potentially abusive mate. The following case is an extreme example of this destructive urge:

A policeman hired someone to make what became an ill-fated attempt to murder his wife. He was sentenced to five years' probation. One reason for the lenient punishment was that his wife pleaded on his behalf and assured the court that she planned to resume living with him.

While not all cases are this extreme, the question must be asked why people are attracted to certain people and why they remain with the ones that they do. Early life experiences are

171

probably the most powerful determinants of such behavior.

Social pressures and cultural realities also make it difficult for such relationships to end. Society still makes it hard for the marginally adjusted woman to remove herself from abusive situations. Some women may find it difficult to press legal charges against their mates because of fears of physical retribution and because of an unresponsive legal system.

Traditionally, it is still felt in some parts of the country that what goes on in the home is no one else's business, that "private" problems should be handled privately. Historically, a certain amount of force in the home, usually against women and children, has been "officially" condoned, as when a judge acquitted a deputy sheriff of wife-beating, saying that abuse was a "normal everyday standard of conduct" for the couple.

Such attitudes are unfortunate, and sexism may make it hard for women to find adequate relief from violence. However, to consider sexism the primary cause of spouse abuse is an oversimplification of a very complex problem.

## COMMON REACTIONS
## TO SPOUSE ABUSE

Violence always arouses a panoply of responses. It is so emotionally stimulating that many of these reactions are often unconsciously designed to calm the observer rather than help the participants. Usually the danger is distorted in one way or another. This will obviously not be of much use to those involved in abuse. Therefore, characteristic responses to spouse abuse should be recognized and understood if potentially lethal outcomes are to be diminished.

The following are some of the more common reactions to spouse abuse with an explanation why these occur:

1. *Deny the existence of spouse abuse.* This most common reaction serves to protect the observer from the anxiety of discov-

ering the presence of abuse. If abuse doesn't exist, then nothing needs to be done about it. A variant of this response is the belief that even if abuse exists, its magnitude is exaggerated, usually by the victim. The reverse is more generally true; abuse is usually under-, not over-, reported. People tend to hide or minimize what is happening because of shame, guilt, or fear. Thus, any report or evidence of violence should be taken very seriously.

2. *Get angry at the perpetrator or victim.* People who are involved in spouse abuse may unconsciously encourage others to get angry at them, metaphorically to beat them. Such people are covertly provocative and the observer may quickly be drawn into this destructive mode of interaction. When the observer becomes aware of this, it can serve as good evidence for some of the underlying psychological and long-standing issues involved in abuse.

3. *Blame abuse on a sexist society.* Simplistic notions that abuse is the result of sexism and little else dooms any intervention to failure. In ignoring lifelong histories of poor self-esteem, abuse, mutual provocation, and the fact that men as well as women are often victims, a unidimensional theory is used to explain a multidimensional problem. An observer with this reaction is uncomfortable with the realization that some people play a part in being beaten; that, for some, there is unconscious gratification in pain.

4. *Blame women who are abused and call them masochistic.* This predominantly male response indicates that the observer is uncomfortable with his own sadistic impulses and thus wants to blame the victim for the abuse. The term masochism is often misused and its meanings misunderstood. Some victims are willing accomplices, others not. Both men and women can be masochistic. In any case, masochism is not an *excuse* for violence. It is a label for unconscious wishes for punishment in order to exculpate oneself or in order to repeat and recapture earlier relationships. People who are abused don't do well because they feel that they don't deserve to do well. However, to rely solely on the concept of masochism is to neglect other

173

important factors: for instance, the abuser's wish to get revenge, and consequent sadistic behavior in righting past, perceived, parental wrongs. Those who explain spousal violence by saying it is entirely the result of masochism also ignore society's role in condoning and perpetuating these relationships once they begin.

5. *Agree that women deserve to be beaten and, if they "step out of line," put in their place.* Cultural expectations certainly influence the occurrence and expression of violence. However, this response indicates that the observer is frightened of the intensity of violence that occurs in spouse abuse and therefore is attempting to minimize it by rationalizing it away; calling it due to machismo, for instance. Such a response also indicates that the observer's self-esteem is easily threatened, since a beating for "stepping out of line" is clearly an overreaction and inappropriate. The control of others in order to enhance one's self-worth is a clear sign of difficulty. In addition, this response may also indicate that the observer was abused or neglected as a child, since people with such a history frequently feel *that violence is appropriate* and is usually deserved.

6. *Become convinced that abuse is only a lower-class phenomenon.* "It's not me" who can be violent, "it's only them." This denial, a typical middle-class response, can be lethal. Abuse will likely go undetected; "It can't be happening here." Such a bias is one of the reasons why medical personnel who are also members of the middle class are such poor case finders. Spousal violence is common to *all* social groups.

7. *Label spousal violence as a marital dispute* whose differences should be solved in the home without the interference of others. This may be reasonable if the argument is nonviolent. But the response is usually a denial of what the observer suspects to be true. Who wants to confront violence in a neighbor, family member, or friend?

8. *Call spouses who resort to violence mentally ill.* This is another form of distancing and denial: only "crazy" people are violent, not "normal people like us." Certain illnesses do indeed weaken impulse control, thus increasing the likelihood of vio-

lence. However, the majority of people involved in abuse are not suffering from the mental illnesses that are associated with being "crazy." In fact, those involved in abuse appear on the surface to be normal.

## THE ABUSIVE MATRIX
## INCREASED RISK OF VIOLENCE

Some people never participate in violence; others do so only when under extreme stress; and still others resort to violence in consistent and continuous ways. It is difficult, if not impossible, to predict *who* actually will be violent, *when* and *how*. However, certain findings are usually present when violence occurs. These are the characteristics of the abusive matrix. Violence rarely occurs "out of the blue" and the following factors are frequently present:

• *A past history of violence or exposure to violence in childhood.* People who witnessed parental violence are more likely to repeat this behavior as adults. Battered children, too, become battering or battered spouses.

A history of trouble with the law, fights resulting in hospitalization, use of weapons, killing someone (including in the military), and problems with authority are all high-risk factors. Other indicators of possible difficulties with impulse control are frequent accidents (especially involving automobiles), a poor military record, or many job changes. The triad of childhood fire-setting, bedwetting, and cruelty to animals has been reported in those particularly prone to adult violence.

• *Feelings of low self-esteem, powerlessness, and dependence.* If someone feels secure, violence is rare. Violence is resorted to in order to repair wounded pride or to protect against loss. For example, excessive jealousy and overpossessiveness are frequent symptoms. Abusive spouses often do not let their mates do much on their own for fear of losing them. When such partners make moves toward independence, violence may

175

result. Victims, too, feel that they are powerless to change their lives, that they deserve what they get, and that no one else would have them.

• *Social isolation and lack of social supports.* A spouse already overwhelmed is less capable of dealing with the difficulties of everyday life without the help of others. But people involved in abuse are ashamed and unwilling to let others know what actually is going on. They do not expect help, since they were not helped as children. A lack of social support is frequently found in those prone to violence.

• *A history of drug abuse, particularly alcoholism.* Alcohol loosens inhibitions and makes it more likely, for someone so disposed, to become aggressive or the victim of violence. People may blame alcohol for the violence, but this is just another form of denial. "It only happens when I'm drunk" means that it will happen again. Alcohol is used as an excuse for action. Other drugs, particularly amphetamines, can be associated with dangerous behavior. Substances are also used as a form of self-medication in order to soothe the participants once the violence has passed. Whatever the case, excessive drug or alcohol use is cause for alarm.

• *The presence of illnesses that affect thinking.* Illnesses that interfere with the ability to think make violence more likely. An ill brain is erratic and unreliable; judgment is diminished and behavior is less mature. At times the presence of a physical illness is overlooked. All that may be apparent are the behavioral changes, while the underlying physical disorders are not diagnosed:

Over a nine-year period, a forty-seven year old account executive became irritable, experienced temper outbursts, and made accusations of infidelity against his wife. He began carrying a pistol and on occasion threatened her with it. Eventually, a slow-growing but fatal brain tumor was diagnosed.

The presence of any psychotic illness accompanied by a break with reality increases the risk of destructive behavior, especially when patients are experiencing voices telling them to hurt themselves or someone else.

• *The presence of a provocative victim.* This is an extremely high-risk factor, especially if the victim also has suicidal thoughts. It is not uncommon for such a person to try to get someone else to do him or her in. Provocation can easily lead to death. For instance, people may provoke a mate into shooting them. Some people attack police with this in mind.

## DANGER SIGNALS
## CLUES TO SPOUSE ABUSE

Given the presence of the abusive matrix, what are the danger signals that violence is about to occur or actually is occurring? During the abusive crisis, victims and perpetrators often withdraw from their usual activities and social contacts, thus keeping their difficulties from view. However, there are many clues available to friends, families, and physicians, if they are willing to recognize them.

As with the other maladaptive behaviors, spouse abuse is resorted to as a destructive solution to circumstances that feel as if they are outside of the participant's control and represents a misguided attempt to reestablish homeostasis. The actual phase of violence is time-limited. It is preceded by a variable period of tension build-up that may be characterized by the usual symptoms of stress. Postviolence behavior is marked by tension reduction. The participants may then engage in intimate contact and mutual denial that this cycle will be repeated. Therefore, the clues to violence depend on which part of the cycle the couple is in. The following are the major danger signals to look for in order to diagnose the presence of spouse abuse:

• *Threats of violence* should always be taken seriously. Certainly, many are not carried out, but such threats always have some meaning and are indications of severe distress. Plans for "revenge" and for "getting even" are particularly ominous.

177

• *An increase in jealousy and accusations of infidelity* is cause for alarm particularly if accompanied by intense and even paranoid overpossessiveness. The spouse, man or woman, may be unwilling to let the other out of sight and may be extremely suspicious of infidelity. Such people are so sensitive to implied or actual slights that they react violently to any humiliation or threat of loss, real or imagined.

• *Victims and perpetrators of spouse abuse develop various psychosomatic concerns* that are related to the anxiety and depression experienced during the build-up phase preceding the actual abuse. Following a beating, victims of abuse also come to physicians with these vague complaints. Suffering physically, they will not mention the abuse and violence unless queried directly. Because these people are likely to visit a number of physicians or emergency rooms, they may gather an arsenal of psychoactive drugs that may later come into play in suicide attempts.

• *The presence of physical trauma,* no matter what the explanation, can be the result of spousal violence. Injuries to the face, breasts, and arms are most common in abuse, but any sort of injury can occur. "Accidents" and explanations of "falling" or "bumping into" things must be examined critically. Because of fear and shame, most victims will give conventional excuses when first asked, but most will admit abuse when pressed. Unfortunately, the observer's wish to deny the existence of violence is so strong that the first, easy explanation is frequently accepted.

• *Any unusual difficulties during the prepartum period* can be a clue to abuse and also indicate a high-risk family for child abuse and neglect. Therefore, a history of miscarriages or spontaneous abortions, anxiety, or other behavioral changes during the pregnancy are indications for further psychosocial investigations.

• *Behavioral problems* in children, such as bedwetting, temper tantrums, nightmares, truancy from school, excessive tiredness in school, promiscuity, or other antisocial behavior should alert the observer to problems elsewhere in the family and to the possibility of spouse abuse. Children of such families may suffer from multiple psychosomatic complaints as well.

## WHAT THEY SAY
## WHAT THEY MEAN

Even when abuse is suspected, participants often deny, minimize, or in other ways deflect attention from their predicament. The following are some of the more common statements that are made, followed by what such statements really mean.

| *Says* | *Means* |
|---|---|
| I wonder what I did wrong to deserve this? | I have been miserable my whole life. When I was young I thought that was my fault. I think the same thing today. |
| He only hits me when he's drunk. | The problem is greater than just being drunk, but it frightens me to think that he would do those things on purpose. However, I feel helpless to change. |
| He only hit me once or twice. | I am very frightened. He beats me regularly with his fists, belt, shoes—with anything he can get hold of. |
| It is safe for me to go home. | I know that it will happen again but I am frightened to live by myself. |

179

| *Says* | *Means* |
|---|---|
| I won't do it again. | It is hard for me to talk about why I resort to violence so easily. I get frightened that I will be left all alone, but I am ashamed to tell anyone about this fear. |
| No one can help me. | Abuse is a way of life for me. I never was helped as a child. I don't trust anyone to help me now. Though I see that you are trying to be useful, it is hard for me to believe that anything good can come of it. |

## GENERAL APPROACHES TO THE ABUSIVE SITUATION

Samuel Butler's dictim, that "Silence is not always tact and it is tact that is golden, not silence," is applicable here. Once abuse is discovered or suspected, there are various options open to concerned family, friends, or physicians. Some are more tactful than others. But something must be done. The following is a sampling of some incorrect maneuvers. More helpful approaches follow.

### Commonly Made Errors

*Action:* Do nothing and hope that the problem goes away.

*Result:* Violence usually continues unless there is a radical change in the abuser-abused relationship. Most participants in spousal violence are convinced that they are beyond help.

To ignore them and their difficulties will only confirm this view and make them feel even more isolated and hopeless. Social support and an impetus for change are necessary.

*Action:* Tell the victim that everything will be all right—the abuser is just having a "bad day."

*Result:* Empty reassurances make victims feel even more isolated and helpless. They realize (correctly) that the observer is too uncomfortable with the problem to be of any use. Feeling rejected by such a "brush-off," victims are less likely to seek further help; they will expect more of the same. The victim's sense of reality may also be further distorted by this lack of validation, since, in fact, everything is all wrong. Victims need external assurance that they do not deserve to be beaten.

*Action:* Tell the couple that their behavior is embarrassing and that they must change immediately.

*Result:* Immediate change is neither possible nor realistic. Since these couples find it especially difficult to alter their behavior, they will feel as if they let the observer down, leading to further shame and social withdrawal. Violence is the result of deeply ingrained character traits, low self-esteem, an inability to tolerate frustration, and feelings of humiliation. Since both people are usually emotionally needy, the attachment between abusive people is often both intense and ambivalent. To expect rapid change only leads to failure.

*Action:* Threaten the abuser with the police.

*Result:* The abuser may appear to comply, but the violence will erupt again once the threat of external intervention is over. In addition, threats serve to further humiliate the perpetrator, thus increasing the likelihood of violent action. Abusers when cornered may precipitate attempts at saving face. Threats in the name of authority have little positive effect, since so many of these people have lived with threats throughout their lives. However, police may need to be called if danger is imminent.

181

*Action:* Tell the couple that marriage is "sacred." They have a moral obligation to work things out.

*Result:* This approach creates another social impediment that must be overcome if their lives are to be more tolerable. When separation or divorce are not alternatives, participants in spousal violence will feel more trapped than ever, increasing their sense of helplessness and danger. Some couples are told that they should stay together "because of the children." This is wrong, since children of such marriages are often abused and neglected too and are candidates for spousal violence.

*Action:* Side with either the perpetrator of the victim in order to "prove" that the abuse is the fault of the other.

*Result:* Attempting to place blame creates a witch-hunt atmosphere and ignores the mutual fit and provocation commonly found in most abusive situations. A judgmental, punitive approach reinforces the notion that the world is an unsympathetic place to live in for the nonaligned participant. Finding fault merely inflames the situation. The advice to "get even" may escalate abuse into homicide.

## Helpful General Interventions

A nonjudgmental approach is best, since both the victim and abuser feel ashamed and easily humiliated; thou shalts and shalt nots feel like further attacks, which they are. However, the ability to be totally even-handed is illusory—it is a desired, if unreachable, ideal.

If the urge to do a solo "rescue" is overwhelming, introspection is in order. An attempt to rescue rather than realistically approach those involved in abusive situations usually fails, since the realities of the situation are generally overlooked. Assistance and advice can be sought from local agencies involved in the treatment of abuse, safehouses (women's shelters), psychiatrists, mental health centers, and clergy. If the danger is high, then the police should be called.

Help should be sought immediately when: 1) there is actual

violence occurring; 2) there is a high risk of imminent violence; 3) there is immediate danger of one of the other maladaptive behaviors, for example, suicide or child abuse; or 4) when the observer has a hunch that something is very wrong. Such intuition is often an excellent barometer of danger. An overreaction is better than no reaction at all.

If abuse is not obvious but suspected, it is best to ask direct questions. For example, "Have you been fighting with each other?" "Are you frightened of hurting or being hurt by your spouse?" are appropriate. Do not worry that those who are questioned will be insulted. They are more likely to be reassured by the concern.

Do not be put off by initial denials of abuse. Once the abuser and / or abused are convinced that friends and family want to help, aspects of the true story will emerge. Remember that many of these people do not feel that they *deserve* help and they feel guilty getting it. If the denial persists, continue with direct inquiry at another time.

Other useful interventions are:

• When the danger is judged to be high, couples should be separated, if necessary by force, for a cooling-off period. For example, safe houses and relatives' and friends' homes can be utilized for this purpose.

• If the danger of abuse is immediate, then police should be called to intervene. The time of intervention can be very dangerous. Couples not uncommonly turn on their "rescuers" and many police deaths occur in just this situation. Therefore, it is important for others who are not trained in dealing with physical violence to avoid directly confronting a physical fight. This could place the observer in extreme danger.

• Access to weapons must be prohibited even during times of decreased crisis. Homicide may result if the means are present. Therefore, it is useful to ask about the presence of weapons and to try to convince the couple to remove them from the house.

• Legal interventions can be helpful in extending the cooling-off period. Restraining orders that prevent the abuser from returning home can provide time for calmer heads to prevail. Legal advice can be obtained privately or through legal aid agencies. Furthermore, women's shelters will also be able to refer people to attorneys who specialize in domestic law.

• Mental health interventions can be accomplished by contacting a private psychiatrist, university hospitals, or a mental health center in the community. For example, some couples may be able to utilize emergency psychiatric interventions and crisis treatment that can be provided by such agencies. Hospitals and mental health centers usually have twenty-four-hour emergency services available, and it is best to seek help for abusive couples at the time that they will accept it, even if it is in the middle of the night. In the morning they may change their minds.

• Reports to the local child protection teams located through child welfare agencies may be necessary if there are children in the home. Although child abuse does not always coexist with spousal violence, the chances are greater in such families and exposure to parental violence is in itself a form of emotional abuse. Such patients are frequently overwhelmed by the responsibilities of parenthood and need whatever professional help is forthcoming.

• The provision of emotional support to either the victim or perpetrator can be extremely useful if either one is attempting to change. For example, the victim may attempt financial independence, go to school, find a job, decrease alcohol consumption, enter psychotherapy, and so forth. These moves toward maturity should be encouraged but also are a time of danger if the other partner views the changes as a desertion. Therefore, if one mate gets better more quickly than the other, there is an increased danger of abusive behavior or suicide in the one who feels left behind.

# THE MEDICAL EVALUATION
# OF SPOUSAL VIOLENCE

Victims of abuse are uncomfortable about seeking medical attention. They may fear public shame and further violence if their spouse feels betrayed. Such people see doctors because of "accidental" trauma or because of somatic ills that are the result of anxiety and depression. Perpetrators also suffer from the symptoms of stress and not infrequently seek medical help. Therefore, there are multiple medical opportunities to intervene in spousal violence.

The following are some of the mistakes more commonly made by physicians, followed by some suggested helpful interventions.

## Commonly Made Medical Errors

*Action:* See the victim and perpetrator together, not individually.

*Result:* A frequent clue to abuse is a mate who seems reluctant to leave the other spouse alone with the physician. In all likelihood the victim will be too frightened or embarrassed to speak in front of the tormentor. This may be exactly what the physician unconsciously wants, because of his own discomfort with violence. ALL couples with ANY complaint should be seen both separately and together in order to allow the physician to judge their mode of interaction as well as to allow the couple to talk of private matters.

*Action:* Avoid questioning the patient. Accept inconsistent and false explanations for the presence of trauma.

*Result:* Staying away from "personal" areas covertly tells the patient that the physician is too uncomfortable to deal with such subjects, thus increasing the patient's sense of shame and isolation. People are relieved to find doctors who care enough to move beyond presenting complaints to what is truly both-

185

ering them. Patients will answer most questions if they are asked. A complete psychosocial history garnered by the physician can be a source of great relief.

*Action:* Prescribe antianxiety or antidepressant drugs to patients before an adequate psychosocial evaluation is performed.

*Result:* Patients who are involved in abusive situations are also at a high risk for suicide. Therefore, before any medicine is prescribed, all the violence syndromes must be evaluated and lethality judged in any patient who appears to be under stress, anxious, or depressed.

## Helpful Medical Interventions

All of the danger syndromes must be considered. Difficult questions should not be avoided. The patient should be asked directly about thoughts of violence, suicide, abuse, and problems with alcohol. Patients can be asked, for example, "Do you have trouble with your temper?" "Does anyone in your family have trouble with theirs?" "I know you may be ashamed of what happened, but could it be that this injury did not happen by accident?"

The patient should be observed for:

• *Trauma,* especially of the head, face, eyes, arms, and breasts. Examine for trauma in different stages of healing. Have the patient undress completely—otherwise, covert trauma can be missed. Patients often will say "I fell" or "I bumped into a door." These explanations should be challenged when the doctor feels he has developed a rapport with the patient.

• *Be alert for symptoms and signs of tension:* depression, anxiety, problems with sleep, nightmares, bodily concerns, trouble with appetite, and so forth. A history of suicide attempts can be a clue to spouse abuse.

• *A history of repeated visits to hospitals,* clinics, or emergency rooms should not be written off only as abuse of the system. This can be a clue to an underlying dysfunctional state where violence is a definite possibility. Many patients make multiple visits before the true nature of their difficulties is discovered.

• Ascertain whether there were any *unusual problems during pregnancy* or a history of miscarriages or abortions.

If there is indication of the presence of any one of the violence syndromes, then an immediate psychiatric consultation must be obtained—especially if lethality is judged to be high. The psychiatric evaluation is designed to determine the level of lethality and to initiate emergency treatment interventions.

## EMERGENCY PSYCHIATRIC INTERVENTIONS

Victims and perpetrators of abuse are evaluated psychiatrically in many different situations—for example, when they come to emergency rooms or after they are seen by other physicians or the police. Before patients can receive adequate emergency care, a number of errors must be avoided, the primary one being the denial of the true and immediate danger faced by the abusive couple. Mental health professionals collude in this denial and therefore may underestimate the potential for danger. Finding out that abuse has occurred is not enough. Therapists may minimize the *intensity* of the violence and therefore the potential lethality.

### Commonly Made Psychiatric Errors

*Action:* Avoid asking specific details about the abuse.

*Result:* An incomplete evaluation may lead to the death of the victim, since the true danger of abuse will become apparent only by asking in *explicit detail* what has occurred. Therapists frequently avoid asking about weapons, homicidal thoughts, trouble with the law, or other specific indicators of violence. This denial of violence lowers the therapist's anxiety

187

and incorrectly supports the idea that nothing is seriously wrong. Therapists will frequently fail to ask about weapons— who wants to be in a room with someone who has murderous impulses and is carrying a gun? But is it better not to know? Lethality can never be judged correctly without finding out *exactly* what has occurred and *what is planned* for the future.

*Action:* Focus only on the problems of spousal violence.

*Result:* The therapist may wish to think that the only problem is spouse abuse, but the entire family needs evaluation for all the danger syndromes if further violence is to be avoided.

*Action:* Tell the patient to leave the perpetrator.

*Result:* Giving advice is *not* psychotherapy; maximizing the *patient's* adaptive and healthy maneuvers and solutions to the problem is. If this demand is unrealistic or at least immediately unattainable in the patient's view, the patient's sense of failure will be increased. A patient advised to leave a mate (whether the abuser or abused) may not return for the next appointment on the assumption that the clinician will be angry that he or she did not live up to the clinician's expectations. Giving such advice to victims indicates that the clinician does not have a clear idea about the mutuality of such abusive relationships, and may be dangerously underestimating the victim's self-destructive potential.

*Action:* See a potentially dangerous patient alone, in a small room with little help available.

*Result:* Another subtle form of denying the potential for violence is overlooking one's own anxiety about it, and this may place the clinician in danger. Some clinicians do not take necessary precautions when seeing potentially dangerous patients; they don't want to acknowledge the danger. This will make many patients feel unsafe, since such violent patients are often covertly asking for external controls and acknowledgment of their dangerousness. If they feel that they are not being taken seriously, their behavior may escalate until someone responds appropriately. For example:

A huge, threatening patient was seen in a small interviewing room alone, with the door closed. He said he was going to kill his wife. The therapist spoke of the subject by using the indefinite "*If* you kill your wife, then you will get into trouble," and so forth. The patient became more and more agitated with this dismissal of his intent until the therapist used the more definite "when." With this recognition of his dangerousness, the patient began to calm down, since he knew he was being taken seriously.

## Helpful Emergency Psychiatric Interventions

Two goals should be kept in mind when dealing with violent situations: the reduction of *immediate* danger and the creation of an environment that permits *long-term change*. Violence is episodic and the period of highest lethality lasts only a short time. The time of physically destructive behavior is only one small part of the cycle of abuse. However, this is when danger is greatest. Therefore, any intervention, at the very least, must be designed to decrease the chances of injury. Of immediate concern, then, is people's physical safety.

In order to avoid developing a nihilistic outlook about long-term prognosis major character change should not be expected immediately. In fact, abusive couples frequently move from crisis to crisis involving friends, family, and physicians but make little effort at meaningful change between times of turmoil. This chronic course should be expected. Eventually, couples might make healthy moves, but usually only after a series of maladaptive behaviors has been lived through. Such a "revolving door" approach to treatment provides sanctuary for couples during times of crisis but does not burden them with unrealistic expectations. Eventually, a certain percentage will make those expectations their own.

Victims or perpetrators should be seen in private without the mate present so that a proper history can be obtained. Remember that some victims fear returning home to another beating if the spouse feels betrayed. Therefore, all the information should be held in strictest confidence, including the very fact of being seen. The only time that such confidentiality should be broken is if there is an imminent danger of homicide, suicide, or child abuse.

In addition to the points in the general and medical sections, other areas to be explored are:

• What triggers the actual abusive behavior? These sources of stress should be identified and alternative responses encouraged. Can the participants find a less maladaptive way to cope? For example, a woman who felt insecure about her husband's love complained bitterly when he went on business trips:

It felt to the woman that she was being deserted. Their arguments became so intense that, on occasion, her husband hit her, once bruising her eye and cutting her lip. During an initial psychiatric examination, it became obvious to the patient and therapist that this feeling of desertion resonated with the patient's earlier experience of parental neglect. Her father had deserted the family when she was eight and she was frightened that her husband would do the same. She had unconsciously equated both men. This realization allowed her to feel less anxious about her husband's absences. The patient entered long-term psychotherapy in order to explore further the effects of her early experiences. Her husband, too, sought psychotherapeutic assistance.

• What are the specifics of the violence? If the patient was beaten, how often and with what? Were fists or an open hand used? Was either the victim or perpetrator ever hospitalized because of violence? Were there ever any broken bones? What were the couple's early childhood experiences? How violent? This will give a clue to how violent they are capable of being now.

• Are homicidal or suicidal ideation present in either the victim or perpetrator? Perpetrators can be suicidal, while victims are frequently homicidal. Are there children in the home? How are they being treated? In addition, abused spouses may also abuse their own parents.

• Are there weapons in the house, in the car, or otherwise available? Were they recently purchased? Have either the abuser or the abused threatened anyone with these weapons even in jest? Access to weapons must be prohibited as one of the first steps in emergency care.

• Is either person using alcohol or drugs? Are other factors present that decrease impulse control, such as other stresses, physical illness, or mental disorders?

• Can family or friends be relied on for assistance for emergency placement in order to separate the victim, perpetrator, and children? The victim may also be given the names and addresses of community agencies involved in the treatment of domestic violence. Legal services, women's shelters, support groups, alcohol and drug treatment centers, and child care centers all have a place in emergency treatment. If the spouse abuse is significant and children are present, then the case must be given to child welfare for further evaluation.

The task of the emergency evaluation is to decrease the chances of physical danger. Change in patterns of family interactions and individual participation in violence can only be accomplished with long-term psychiatric help, including individual psychotherapy, groups, couple's treatment, and family meetings. Chronic patterns of abuse and violence must be uncovered, and issues of self-esteem, depression, dependency, and guilt dealt with in the victim and perpetrator if other, less maladaptive behaviors are to be adopted. How-

191

ever, those involved in abuse rarely enter such treatment immediately. Unfortunately, most live through a number of destructive cycles before permanent moves toward health are made.

# 6

# Suicide

I take it that no man is educated who
has never dallied with the thought
of suicide.

*William James*

The suicide crisis develops slowly. Even with planning, the actual lethal act may occur impulsively, at the end of a build-up phase that can last for weeks or months. The majority of suicidal people want to be stopped, at least at some level, and therefore give indirect clues to their intentions. For a variety of reasons, these indicators are often overlooked or actively ignored, as can be seen in the case of Mr. E., a fifty-seven-year-old construction worker and ex-deep sea diver.

He returned to his physician about two months after a chicken bone was removed from his esophagus. He complained that something was "still stuck inside." He wondered if he would ever get better. An X-ray was done and was normal. Because he also complained of insomnia, sleeping pills were prescribed.

Mr. E. felt somewhat better for a few days, but he had

193

another relapse following a violent coughing fit. Mrs. E. felt anxious about her husband's declining health, his problems at work, and the household finances.

Mr. E. tried to return to work but became dizzy when walking on the high girders. His back hurt in the morning. He developed headaches. His previously excellent work record was being marred by near-accidents, declining productivity, and frequent absences. His foreman suggested that he take some more time off.

Mr. E. became more irritable at home and fearful that the neighborhood was "turning bad." He purchased a handgun "in case" someone tried to rob them. He said that he didn't know what he would do if his health didn't improve. Mr. E. also mentioned that perhaps "the family would be better off" without him. After a particularly loud argument with his daughter, he went up to the bedroom and put the loaded gun to his mouth.

After telling his wife what happened, she told him to "forget" about his health and go back to work. Mr. E. felt that his wife didn't understand how badly he felt, continued to complain of various aches and pains, and made another appointment to see his doctor. The morning of his appointment he told Mrs. E. jokingly that he was going to buy some "dumdum" bullets for his gun. He hoped that the doctor was going to "cut out" whatever was inside, and he said that he couldn't "take this much longer."

The doctor met with both Mr. and Mrs. E. after a normal physical examination was performed. He asked how things were at home. Mr. E. said things were going fine, and Mrs. E. did not contradict him. The questioning stopped here.

However, while leaving the office Mrs. E. told the receptionist about her husband's bullets. The physician called the patient and a psychiatric consultation was obtained. Mr. E. was admitted to a psychiatric unit where the diagnosis of severe depression was made. With

194

appropriate treatment his symptoms improved, his physical concerns and suicidal thoughts dissipated, and he returned to work six weeks later.

People are frequently in active medical treatment during the suicide crisis. In fact, in some studies, over 50 percent of patients see their physician in the month before they die, 80 percent in the six months before death. Furthermore, physicians inadvertently supply the means for suicide by prescribing potentially lethal amounts of sleeping medicines, tranquilizers, or antidepressants to covertly suicidal patients. Many patients do not speak directly of their wish to die but rather, like Mr. E., give clues to their intentions—for example, with offhand comments, or by complaining to their doctor or family of symptoms of depression or tension. Even if highly lethal, most suicidal people are ambivalent about dying. They give many indirect indications that they want to be stopped. Family, friends, and physicians—because of ignorance, antipathy, or anxiety—overlook opportunities for early interventions or do not intervene at all.

Why was Mr. E.'s distress ignored until almost too late? He gave many clues as to his frame of mind. Early in his illness he developed symptoms that were due to an undiagnosed depression; he was irritable, had trouble sleeping, had temper outbursts, developed various physical ills usually associated with stress, began to ruminate about his poor health, and generally became a complainer when before he seemed quite self-reliant. Mr. E.'s irritability and general lack of good humor was probably one reason why his physician did not pay more attention to his obvious downhill course. Because of his changed disposition it was difficult for anyone to spend much time with Mr. E.; the doctor was no exception.

Physicians don't like to ask about suicidal behavior. Some erroneously believe that asking about it can suggest it to the patient. Some physicians feel that they have neither the time nor the training to deal with the suicidal patient; therefore, if they don't ask and don't find problems, it doesn't exist. What

195

if the patient says yes? What does the doctor do then? Furthermore, doctors have a difficult time with death; they are taught that to cure is divine and death is a symptom of defeat. Physicians become angry at patients who are suicidal, since they are trying to die "on purpose" and not from some disease that the doctor feels is outside of the patient's control. Some feel that suicidal patients are not "really" sick. They are just "creating" their illness to seek attention. Finally, suicidal patients may remind physicians uncomfortably of their own self-destructive impulses.

Families and friends react similarly. They may even be relieved to be rid of the patient, especially if the situation has been draining or difficult. They may act as if to say "stop complaining and threatening. . . . Do it already." Hopelessness is a central feature of suicide. Everything looks black; the victim cannot be dissuaded from this outlook no matter what the realities. Mr. E. thought he never would get better. And this hopelessness is transmitted to family, friends, and physicians. Such hostile responses to suicidal people are also understandable if it is realized that suicidal behavior frequently involves covert hostility toward others. It is no accident that suicidal people make others angry. It is not surprising that there may be some relief to see them go. Such "death wishes" in others must be acknowledged if they are to be effectively dealt with and not acted upon. Because Mrs. E. was fed up with her husband, she neglected to tell the physician about the gun and recently purchased bullets. Luckily she mentioned them to the receptionist in passing.

## AMBIVALENCE

Most suicidal people are ambivalent about death. Those who have survived bullets to the head and jumps from great heights describe wishes to be stopped and fantasies that they will be saved even while falling or pulling the trigger. Thoughts of reunion, immortality, revenge, or cheating death—or of watching one's funeral—also support the notion that many people don't really believe they will die even while using a highly lethal method. The notion of ambivalence is also supported by the fact that at least 80 percent of successful suicides leave clues to their intentions. Mr. E. made a number of indirect references to feelings of hopelessness about his illness and gave ample indications about suicidal ideation. People kill themselves, however, no matter how ambivalent they are. Sometimes, like Mrs. A. in the following example, they misjudge their dose or chosen method and die, perhaps by mistake.

Mrs. A., a twenty-nine-year-old schoolteacher and mother of two children, was first involved with self-destructive activity when she was brought by ambulance to a large city hospital after ingesting a bottle of sleeping pills. She was comatose and able to breathe only with the help of artificial respiration. The fluid from her stomach contained fragments of many pills.

She was admitted to the medical intensive care unit, where she slowly regained consciousness. She was examined by a psychiatrist who determined that although Mrs. A. was still depressed and potentially suicidal, the acute danger had passed. The psychiatrist did not speak with her family or friends, and Mrs. A. was told she was free to leave the hospital. No one understood why she had taken the pills, what problem she was trying to solve by this behavior. She refused referral for outpatient psychiatric care.

Four weeks later she was brought to another emergency room following a second overdose, this time with highly lethal antidepressants. She died in the emergency room.

Mrs. A. was the youngest of three girls born to a housewife mother and a schoolteacher father. Her father was prone to bouts of depression and when Mrs. A. was three years old he left home for a few months for reasons she as a child did not understand. After this she began bedwetting and having nightmares. The latter continued for some time after the father returned home.

When she was eighteen her parents divorced. Shortly thereafter, her father hanged himself. Mrs. A. went "blank" and did not cry at the funeral. Two months later she married and in rapid succession had two children, with a stillbirth in between. She also did not cry when this happened.

The marriage was troubled from the beginning. Mrs. A. did not feel close to her husband. She would at times confuse her husband's name with that of her dead father. Five years after the stillbirth, she experienced a period of sadness, insomnia, anxiety, and a decrease in appetite. She began to have trouble functioning at work. These difficulties passed, but her gynecologist continued to prescribe Seconal for her sleeping problems. Mrs. A.'s social drinking increased. She usually had a glass of wine handy while doing her housework.

Her marriage ended nine years after it had begun. Her problems with sleeping continued; occasionally she would awaken thinking she could hear a baby crying. When told of the situation, her gynecologist increased her sleeping medications and suggested a vacation.

Her drinking increased dramatically. She hoarded her sleeping medications "just in case" things became intolerable. She worried that she would never remarry, felt that she was a failure, and was hurt that her girls preferred living with their father.

Because of her increasing preoccupations, Mrs. A.'s work deteriorated so that her principal asked her to take a leave of absence from school. She was shocked; work was all she had. Feeling she had no alternative, Mrs. A. took an overdose after she sent her children to stay with their father for the weekend. She then called the police, who found her unconscious when they arrived.

Following this hospitalization she saw her gynecologist, who suggested that she see a psychiatrist. She refused, saying that it probably wouldn't help. He began her on amitriptyline, a potent and potentially lethal antidepressant. A week later she heard that her husband was to remarry. That night Mrs. A. overdosed with her antidepressants. Visiting friends arrived too late to bring her to the hospital in time.

How suicidal was Mrs. A., and how adequate was her treatment? She was evaluated by a psychiatrist after her first overdose attempt but did not follow his recommendation for further psychiatric care. It is not known what transpired during that interview. It is not known, for instance, whether either Mrs. A. or the psychiatrist understood the meaning of the overdose or Mrs. A.'s intent. One can speculate that Mrs. A. played down future suicidal plans. Even though this attempt was severe and took planning (for example, she hoarded her sleeping pills), she did call the police. It is not known whether she spoke openly about any fantasies—for example, thoughts of joining her dead father and stillborn child.

Apparently Mrs. A.'s gynecologist thought she was significantly depressed; he prescribed an antidepressant. It is not known whether he evaluated Mrs. A.'s suicidal potential. This would have been particularly important, since antidepressants are highly lethal and are commonly used in overdose attempts. Approximately 15 percent of patients who suffer from depression kill themselves during the course of their illness. Of patients who die of an overdose, 55 percent do so by means of a *single prescription of medication that was obtained within a week of their death.*

By not speaking with her family, the psychiatrist overlooked important information about Mrs. A.'s functional decline. Nor did the psychiatrist call her gynecologist. The psychiatrist may have felt that he could not force Mrs. A. to accept treatment, even though she was obviously depressed.

199

What is clear is that nothing was accomplished by Mrs. A.'s attempt. She returned to the same life situation with little altered by her suicidal behavior.

## LOSS AND DEPRESSION

An inability to cope adaptively with loss or other life events is a major factor in many suicidal crises. Suicide is a self-destructive solution to seemingly insoluble problems. The loss may be of a person, health, status, wealth, or a previously held idea of oneself.

Mrs. A. did not deal well with loss. She was sensitized by her past experiences and was vulnerable to losses in the present. She did not cry at her father's funeral or her child's and did not adequately mourn their deaths. The mysterious departure of her father early in life also probably weakened her abilities to overcome future privations.

What Mrs. A. was trying to accomplish by her overdoses never was understood. What is certain, however, is that the news of her ex-husband's marriage was more than she could take. It is likely that this reawakened painful memories of her miscarriage, the death of her father, and his desertion of her when she was young.

The first indication of a serious problem was the depression Mrs. A. experienced five years after the death of her child. Why she began to feel depressed then is not clear, but people feel sad or blue at holiday times or at anniversaries of losses. Such anniversary reactions are common. Patients may become depressed when they reach the age of someone who died, even though the death may have occurred many years before. Birthdays may also evoke feelings of loss and precipitate depressions in those so prone, particularly in later years.

Had Mrs. A. inherited a biological tendency for depression and suicide from her father? There is a greater risk of suicide in families where other suicides have occurred. Twenty-five percent of successful attempts occur in such families. Little doubt exists that the propensity to develop significant depressions has a genetic component also associated with excessive alcohol intake. Many of Mrs. A.'s symptoms—sleep disturbance, change in appetite, and weight change, feelings of hopelessness and of being no good, coupled with crying spells and suicidal thoughts lasting more than a month—support the diagnosis of a true clinical depression.

Such clinical depression must be distinguished from the normal moods of sadness or the "blues," which are more transient and do not interfere greatly with functioning. The distinction between normal grief that follows a loss and true depression is at times difficult. Grief runs a shorter course, follows an obvious loss, is less functionally disruptive and is not accompanied by strong and long-lasting feelings of hopelessness, guilt, and self-destruction. Clinical depression, on the other hand, is characterized by recurrent episodes and is frequently accompanied by family histories of depression and/or alcoholism.

It must be remembered that suicide and true depression are not always linked. In fact, suicide occurs in many other situations, although depression is the illness with the highest risk of suicide. Mrs. A. clearly suffered from depression. She had a biological propensity for the disease. She was also sensitized to losses by her life history. Other people who become suicidal are not so clearly depressed. Yet these people, too, kill themselves. Frequently they are adolescents. In fact, suicide is one of the leading causes of death among people of this age group, although it may be that depression is not so obvious in this population, since the symptoms of depression in the young are behavioral disturbances rather than changes in mood. Indications of difficulty will be due to problems in school or with the law rather than to crying or sadness.

Two weeks before his mother was to remarry, D., an eighteen-year-old boy, wandered off into the Arapahoe National Forest and blew his brains out with his father's hunting rifle. To do this, he attached a string to the trigger, ran it around a tree, held the rifle between his knees, and inserted the barrel into his mouth. He was found two days later by some hikers. A cassette machine had recorded the whole thing.

D. had been a normal, healthy baby, the second child born to working-class parents, and named after his father. At age two he was hospitalized briefly because of viral encephalitis. When D. was four his father was killed in a hunting accident. D. did not go to the funeral. Since he really didn't understand what dead meant, he assumed that his father would return some day. Afterward, D. would rock himself to sleep and on occasion his mother would find him sleeping on the floor in front of the bedroom door.

The first real indication of serious difficulty occurred when D. was fourteen. He was arrested for shoplifting, but the charges were dropped. Psychotherapy was suggested by a school counselor but was not followed up on. D.'s mother was engrossed in a career and, although concerned about her son, did little more than forbid D. to watch television for a week. At fifteen D. was suspended from school for threatening another boy with a knife.

He began to avoid any real conversation with his mother and spent most of his time in his room, listening to his stereo. At times he went out for long walks in the country; on occasion he had thoughts that he would run into his father.

During the summer of his high-school graduation he was involved in a severe hang-gliding accident, breaking his arm in two places. A few weeks later, D. was stopped for speeding on the way home, but little came of it.

His mother decided to remarry. Plans were being made for the wedding, the house was being sold. In the midst of this he planned a solo hunting trip, which he thought would reduce some of the feelings of anxiety and extreme loneliness that had recently begun to bother him. During an argument with his mother, she accused him of being selfish, only thinking of himself. He, in turn, said that she was betraying his father by getting married. That night the thought of suicide entered D.'s mind. He found this quite comforting and soothing. He began plotting his death.

Loss of a parent or parental figure early in life is not infrequently found in cases of successful suicides. As with Mrs. A., these people often feel vulnerable to losses and thus construct their world to avoid its impact. People who lose a parent early in life are frequently afraid to enter into intimate relationships, since they are unwilling to give up the memory of their parent by replacing it with the reality of a present-day relationship. In this way they do not lay the dead to rest and thus avoid the pain of mourning. Such people may also feel frightened that they will be deserted in the present as they were in the past.

The death of his father was so painful that D. harbored fantasies that he was still alive—and would someday come back, which is not an uncommon thought among those who have trouble grieving. The remarriage of his mother created a double loss. He was about to lose his mother as well as the fantasy that his father would return someday to reconstitute his original family. D. could not accept this. Unconsciously, he went off in search of his father once again and decided to rejoin him and become like him by reenacting his death. By committing suicide he could get back at his mother, too, for making him suffer.

It is interesting to speculate whether D.'s hang-gliding accident and reckless driving were suicide equivalents; was he unconsciously trying to die? Suicidal persons have more automobile accidents than those who are not. Car accidents provide an excellent opportunity for concealing suicidal behavior. Unfortunately, others die in the process. In one study, 25 percent of the suicidal drivers were found to have driven into other vehicles, injuring innocent victims.

Patients who are suicidal die in different ways, either by their own hand, by "accident," or by getting someone else to do it for them. Firearms are used by 50 percent of male suicides and 25 percent of female suicides. More women (33 percent) than men (20 percent) use poisons. Both sexes use hanging equally (20 percent). Certainly, the threat of using a gun seems much more serious than taking a few aspirin— except if the person is convinced that a few aspirin are lethal. Even if a lethal method is chosen, the question must be asked whether the person intends to be discovered. Apparently, D. did not.

An example of the role of hostility as well as the often dyadic nature of suicide is the recording D. left for his mother. He described in great detail what he was doing—he planned for her to hear the shot. It has been said that no one commits suicide who has not wanted, at least unconsciously, to kill another. Many times suicide is coupled with murder, mostly symbolically, but at times in reality.

Suicide and homicide are linked. Homicides may also be disguised suicides. For instance, 20 to 40 percent of all homicide victims induce their attack often taunting the assailant to pull the trigger. People provoke attacks by police, hoping to get killed. Furthermore, people who make homicidal threats are more likely to kill themselves than harm someone else. Therefore, when suicide is suspected, homicidal thoughts must be evaluated and vice versa.

## REVENGE

Victims often want revenge and they commit or threaten suicide to get it. Suicide notes are messages to those who are meant to suffer; they offer rationalization for the act and often contain information about what the victim is so resentful about. D. left a recording of his death; others leave notes about what they are going to do. The following note is remarkable in its scope; no one was meant to escape unscathed:

To Everyone
Mom, Dad, and Bill

Sally, Harry, Betty, Jack, Sonny, Theresa, Hal, Jim, Mark, Jesse, Linda, Debbie, Rhonda, Betty-Lou, Lennie, Dwayne, Cindy, Baby Irv, Sandra, Baby Michelle, Jerry— Mary's baby, Kathy's baby, Vinnie, Jackie, Gary.

I am hoping I will go into a long sleep. Please forgive me, but I have no one and you all have each other. So please stay together. You have more than I ever will so please stay together. Because you have each other I am taking so many pills. I don't care I just keep drinking them, two, three at a time.

I love everyone but no one knows what I am going through.

I love God very much. God forgive me for what I am doing.

If something happens would you please understand that I am under a lot of pressure.

Love,
Betty

It is not clear what Betty's fantasy was—she was going into a "long sleep" and not going to die. Perhaps she didn't want to miss the pain she was inflicting on so many people. She asks for forgiveness while indicating that other people's happiness is a cause of her own distress. She is attempting to use her suffering as a wedge—and to drive it into other people's lives. "I love everyone but no one knows what I am going through." "No one loves me."

This note has a manipulative quality, and much of suicidal behavior is as much an attempt to influence the environment as it is to die. Many attempts, in fact, can be classified as gestures and not true attempts if the intent to die is not present. There are people who, when under stress, speak in the language of suicide. They live their life by threats. They may cut their wrists or take sublethal overdoses. Although these peo-

205

ple are chronically self-destructive, each suicidal act is not meant to be lethal. However, the long-term prognosis is guarded. Because of their angry and demanding behavior, such patients alienate their friends and family and often ultimately die alone, intentionally or by miscalculation. But revenge can be obtained whether or not one dies.

The wish for revenge can be brutal and sadistic. Consider the following onslaught: A young man called his mother and sister. While on the phone he shot himself in the head.

This man made his family feel as helpless as he. No doubt his suicide represented a partial attempt to get back at them. D.'s cassette tape and Betty's suicide note served this function, too.

Suicidal behavior, then, is associated with diverse circumstances and is symptomatic of problems elsewhere in the person's life. Suicide can coexist with other dangerous behaviors and is often resorted to as a way of dealing with these problems. Victims of incest may attempt to terminate the affair by suicide. During the crisis of disclosure of incest, the danger of suicide is high for all concerned. Twenty-five percent of suicidal adolescent girls are frightened of being, or are, pregnant. Victims of rape and other crimes may turn to suicide to ease their pain. Victims of spousal violence resort to suicide as a way out. A significant number of alcohol abusers take their own lives particularly late in the course of their illness, as do sufferers of other emotional illnesses.

A period of mourning and readjustment must take place following a successful suicide. Relatives of people who have committed suicide are at risk to do so themselves. Also, morbidity and mortality from physical illness is increased in the year following the death of a relative, particularly if the survivors become severely depressed. Physicians who treat patients who kill themselves also must come to terms with the event, especially with their feelings of anger, guilt, sadness, and defeat, which are experienced by everyone.

## COMMON REACTIONS TO SUICIDE

The suicidal situation provokes typical responses, including fear, compassion, concern, and anger. These reactions and how they are handled can influence possible successful or tragic outcomes. The following are some of the more frequent reactions, with an explanation why they occur:

1. *Get angry* at suicidal persons. This is frequently hard to acknowledge. Since the suffering is obvious how can one be angry at someone who is in pain? But covert hostility and manipulative behavior underly most suicidal activity and account for an angry response in others. Danger signals will be overlooked and proper help delayed if the underlying antipathy toward suicidal people is ignored.

2. *Deny* suicidal intent. "It was just an accident" or "He didn't mean to do it" covers up the intense feelings that are evoked by suicidal behavior. The observer may feel too guilty, angry, or anxious to acknowledge what is happening.

3. *Have fantasies of rescuing* the suicidal person. Suicidal people often promote such rescue fantasies by indicating "You are the only one who can help me." This is a covert way of saying, "You are responsible for my life." However, if the observer does accept this responsibility and the situation does not improve, then everyone will feel even more angry and hopeless. By attempting to undo someone else's difficulties, by being blackmailed into action, the observer is underestimating the seriousness of the situation.

Certainly, relatives and friends are extremely important in helping suicidal persons regain hope and a sense of mastery. They can provide the necessary "life line." However, recovery must be handled realistically, with professional help, if it is to be successful and long-lasting.

4. *Label threats* of suicide as *manipulations* just to get attention. This is probably true, but people die to get attention. The word "manipulation" used in this sense can become a

rationalization. Manipulative patients can be judged incorrectly as not being potentially lethal. This is a particularly dangerous view, since what appears to be manipulative behavior one moment can become lethal the next, especially if the manipulation does not work. A young man took ten aspirin when his wife threatened to leave him. She called a physician who said this was just an attempt to get attention and that ten aspirin was not a dangerous overdose. However, when the wife left the next day, her husband shot himself in the abdomen, narrowly escaping death.

5. Call suicide an act of *free will*. Often, philosophical questions hide antipathy, especially if the case seems hopeless, particularly difficult to deal with, or if the patient already has antagonized everyone to the point of distraction. With people who are covertly disliked, the "right to die" question is usually raised. The observer is made to feel as hopeless as the patient; unfortunately, this is not always recognized and the patient is abandoned.

One assumption behind the free will aspect of suicide is that suicide is the result of a rational decision rather than a maladaptive solution to a dilemma that seems hopeless. This ignores the ambivalent nature of most suicides, and the fact that the most suicidal patients are seeking relief from intolerable emotions. For instance, such hopelessness is a hallmark of depression. How free is someone's will if he or she is depressed? If the depression is treated, this hopelessness usually disappears. Mental illness is not inimicable to rational thought; however, when people improve or recover, other solutions become more apparent and possible.

Terminal disease is often cited as a situation when suicide becomes "rational." However, in at least some cases, when suicidal terminally ill patients are provided with other means of mastery over their condition and given control of their treatment and lives, suicidal impulses diminish. Terminally ill patients who suffer from clinical depressions may come to better terms with their diseases if treated. The main point here is that no matter how hopeless a situation may appear, circumstances can change and other behaviors can replace suicidal activity. "Rational" suicides do exist, but other alternatives may be submerged by the observer's own depression.

6. *Feel guilty* following a successful suicide. The thought that not enough was done is common in any death, no matter what the circumstances. In fact, suicidal people may want survivors to feel guilty. A guilty response can also be related to the sense of omnipotence involved in rescue fantasies, be they the result of covert "death wishes" felt toward the patient or due to relief that the person is dead. The grieving process is particularly difficult following a suicide because of the often ambivalent relationships that existed before the death.

## THE MATRIX OF SUICIDE HIGH-RISK FACTORS

Once it was thought that suicidal people did not make their plans known and that suicide frequently occurred without warning. It is now recognized that this is not the case and that people at risk for suicide typically share certain characteristics. Becoming familiar with these is helpful in evaluating the seriousness of suicidal communications. For example, women make more gestures, but more men actually are successful. The widowed, separated, or divorced are at a much higher risk than others.

• *Hopelessness* about one's situation and future possibilities is one of the danger signals. Suicide may be an attempt to "master" a situation that seems desperate and out of one's control. What seems hopeless to a depressed person, however, may not to someone who is emotionally well. Comments such as "I'll never get better" or "Things will never be the same" may be ominous.

• *Loss* is intimately associated with suicide. A recent loss, perhaps in combination with memories of past losses, is usually found. Many suicidal patients have lost a parent early in life and present-day losses reawaken old unresolved issues. As mentioned earlier, anniversaries of losses—and holidays, when ruminations about loss are common—may also precipitate suicidal behavior. Suicide may represent an attempted reunion with the lost person or perhaps atonement for sins thought to have been committed toward them. Such suicidal people may be especially sensitive to rejections, real or imagined. A loss—frequently overlooked—is the actual or symbolic loss of the therapist or phsyician. Vacations and absences by health professionals are major sources of stress for some patients. Furthermore, empathic breaks or outright hostility on the part of the doctor will also be experienced as a rejection by the potentially suicidal person.

• The communication of suicidal intent in *older age groups* is extremely serious, since the risk of suicide increases with age, although it is the second leading cause of death in adolescence. This is partially due to the fact that older people have experienced more losses and are more likely to be alone. Furthermore, depression with its increased risk of suicide is a disease of older age.

Two-thirds of the elderly who commit suicide suffer from some chronic physical illness. Loss of physical health often leads to depression, hopelessness, and the thought of suicide as a way out. Difficulties in the doctor-patient relationship or with other caretakers—for example, a nursing home attendant—may also precipitate a suicidal crisis. This is especially so if the patient feels isolated and "given up on" by those in charge of his or her care.

• Of those who die, 25 percent have a *family history* and over 50 percent have a *personal history* of prior suicide attempts. No matter how trivial, a past history of suicidal behavior in self or family places people in a high-risk category. Past suicidal behavior increases the risk for the future, whether it was a "gesture"—a conscious attempt to influence the environment—or an "attempt"—a serious wish to die.

• Many people who kill themselves are suffering from a diagnosable and treatable *mental illness*. The following percentages of patients kill themselves during the course of their disease: affective disorders (depression, manic-depressive illness), 10 to 15 percent; alcoholism, 15 percent; schizophrenia, 10 percent; drug addiction, 10 percent; character disorders, 5 percent. Suicide is more likely to occur early than late in the course of schizophrenia and depression, but it tends to be a late complication of alcoholism. Schizophrenics are particularly vulnerable during the disorganizing beginning stage of their illness or during postpsychotic depressions when they must come to terms with the realities of their chronic disease.

Over half of successful suicides are depressed. However, the degree of depressive symptomatology is not necessarily correlated with lethality. A slightly depressed person may be highly suicidal while a severe depressive may be in no danger. With depression, the highest risk is during the acute episode and six to nine months after improvement.

Anything that increases impulsive behavior raises the chance of suicide. The presence of psychosis (a break with reality accompanied by, for example, hallucinations, delusions, and a profound change in functioning) increases the danger. The psychosis may be "functional" (due to schizophrenia, depression) or the result of physical illnesses such as drug and alcohol intoxication or withdrawal. The most dangerous are patients who experience "command" hallucinations to hurt themselves and do so according to the instructions of voices they hear.

Alcoholism is another disease genetically related to depression and also associated with suicide. Alcohol is a pharmacological depressant that increases the danger of suicide. It also weakens impulse control, and a high percentage of successful suicides have significant blood alcohol levels at the time of death.

• There is a *close association between suicide and other forms of violence and hostility.* This was recognized early. Griesinger wrote in 1867: "Immediately connected with the suicidal

211

impulse is the tendency to injure and destroy other persons or inanimate objects." A *chaotic family* situation or a history of violence, increased accidents or risk-taking behavior is not uncommon among suicidal people. The suicidal person's anger may be directed at strangers, spouses, or children.

• Suicide is now known to be associated with *adolescent turmoil*, behavior disorders, and antisocial behavior, which are symptomatic of underlying depressions. Adolescent alcholism and drug abuse place the victims in especially high-risk categories. This substance abuse must be distinguished, however, from normal experimentation, which is common at this age. One-half of female adolescents who attempt suicide give sexual molestation as one reason for their difficulties. There is a similar finding among adolescent runaways. Incestuous families are at a high risk for suicide.

• *"Death wishes"* in others, usually unconscious, are sometimes found among family, friends, and physicians. Members of the suicidal person's social system may want them "gone," if not dead. People become fed-up, feel helpless with the patient's hopelessness, and may be responding to the covert anger present in suicidal behavior. Such reactions must be honestly appraised and actually searched for if fatal consequences are not to result. For example, the following patient's father was not adequately evaluated for ambivalent feelings toward his son, who was brought to an emergency room following a minor overdose of sleeping pills:

The boy was sent home to be with his father and was to be brought to an outpatient psychiatric clinic the next day. Instead, the father left the boy alone when he went to work. The father "forgot" to remove his loaded pistol from the dresser and the boy fatally shot himself with it before his father returned.

It is well known among professionals that therapist antipathy is *the* major therapeutic problem in dealing with suicidal patients. One psychiatrist "jokingly" told his patients not to

kill themselves in the hospital since "there would be an inves-
tigation, and too much paperwork." The following example
graphically makes this point.

Dr. ____ (a psychiatrist) believed in being direct with
his patients. He once told a former patient . . . a suicidal
young man who had threatened to jump out a window—
"It's up to you, but if you decide you don't want to live,
for God's sake don't jump out the window. You might
fail and end up a cripple, and then you'd be worse. Just
take pills and do a good job." The following year, the
patient took an overdose of barbiturates and died.

*The New Yorker*
*June 8, 1981*

Such feelings are, in fact, to be expected. However, most
family, friends, and physicians manage to control these feelings and do not carry them out.

## IMPENDING SUICIDE

Many [suicidal persons] artfully seize an
opportune moment to put into execution
the resolution long ago taken, but till now
concealed.

*Griesinger, 1867*

Not all people in high-risk categories are in immediate danger of suicide and therefore emergency action may not be
necessary. However, there are some danger signals that dic-
tate the need for immediate intervention. Quick action when
the following are observed is crucial:

• *Sudden calm* in a previously upset person may mean that
the decision to commit suicide has been reached.
• *An increase in self-deprecatory remarks, depression, and sense of*

213

*hopelessness.* Comments like "I don't think things are going to get better" or "I never was any good" should not be taken lightly. This is no time for empty reassurances.

• *Setting one's affairs in order.* Making wills, telling people about plans for "long" trips, giving away possessions, or increasing life insurance coverage are ominous signs.

• *A rupture in social integration* and estrangement from friends, family, or physicians is problematic. A missed or broken appointment by a depressed person is definite cause for alarm.

• *An increase in alcohol or drug intake.* Such behavior indicates a change in functioning and a potential weakening of self-control. Alcohol and certain drugs (sleeping pills, antianxiety agents) are also pharmacological depressants that increase the risk of suicide.

• *The presence of a concrete plan* is extremely dangerous. It is even more serious if some actual physical preparations have been made. Fleeting thoughts of shooting oneself with a gun that is not present are significantly less dangerous than thoughts of overdosing with pills that have been purchased already. The intent of the plan should also be evaluated and not assumed to be benign. For example, some people might think that three aspirin are lethal. These people are highly suicidal though they are not likely to die of this method. Whether a person has thoughts of being discovered and saved during an attempt is also important information. Does the plan call for a retreat to an isolated location or one where there are likely to be people to intervene? Ambivalence about death is often found in the detailed plans of suicidal people. However, people die by mistake. And finally, the ready availability of weapons such as handguns, rifles, and knives can turn a partially formed impulse into a fatal act.

• *Fear or anxiety* about a potentially suicidal person should be heeded even though there may be a lack of hard evidence. Suicidal people may make others feel what they themselves feel. Often this "gut response" is the only clue to underlying difficulties. One's intuition should be trusted.

# WHAT THEY SAY
# WHAT THEY MEAN

The ambivalence of the suicidal person about living or dying often becomes apparent through language. The words used can provide a key to true intentions.

| *Says* | *Means* |
|---|---|
| Doesn't everyone think of suicide? | My suicidal thoughts are frightening me—I have been thinking very seriously about the possibility of killing myself but am embarrassed to tell you about it directly. |
| I'll never get better. | I feel hopeless about my situation. Please don't offer me empty reassurances—instead, realize that I see no way out of my predicament. |
| Nobody cares for me, I'm no good. | I hate myself and assume that everyone hates me too. Suicide is the only way I have of both punishing myself and getting revenge. |
| You can't stop me. | I hope you try. |
| Leave me alone, I want to die. | I feel hopeless and think I have no way out. However, I hope you don't agree with me. Please try to stop me. |

215

| *Says* | *Means* |
|---|---|
| I think I'll be all right. | I hope you don't believe me and that you hear I am uncertain about what will happen. |
| It was just an accident. | I am ashamed to tell you that it really was a suicide attempt. |

## GENERAL APPROACHES
## TO THE SUICIDAL SITUATION

Once the possibility of suicide is apparent, there are a number of things that can be done by family, friends, and clinicians. Some of these maneuvers will be helpful, others less so. The following are some less helpful interventions. The next section contains more reasonable suggestions.

### Commonly Made Errors

*Action:* Reassure the suicidal person that "everything will be all right."

*Result:* Suicidal people usually feel hopeless. They are convinced that they will never get better. Therefore, empty reassurances *do not* work. This approach leads to even further isolation and loneliness because the person feels misunderstood and as though no one is listening. Reassurances can be useful at times but not when designed to keep the person quiet. The person may then feel compelled to escalate the suicidal behavior in a further plea for help. It is helpful to point out that these hopeless feelings will pass but that something needs to be done about them now.

A variation of this approach is to attempt to argue the person out of their symptoms by minimizing their difficulties or telling them that life is worth living. Even though the attention received may be useful, this maneuver will only delay seeking help. Arguing and reassuring indicate primarily that the observer is unwilling to tolerate and recognize the suicidal person's pain.

*Action:* Ignore the suicidal communications in the hope that the problems will right themselves.

*Result:* The prospect of suicide may be frightening to family and friends because of anxiety about their own suicidal impulses. However, suicidal people want to be "discovered." If ignored, they will feel even more misunderstood, hopeless, and unloved. They may interpret this disregard of their signals as a covert wish that they should carry out their suicide plans, which it may well be.

*Action:* Dare the person to do it in order to point out how "silly" he or she is.

*Result:* This sadistic, provocative approach increases the risk both of suicide *and* homicide; the person at risk may kill himself or attack the person who made the dare. Such an approach results from deep antipathy and death wishes in the observer. The impulse to hurt or at least be rid of suicidal persons is normal; to act on such an impulse through taunts obviously increases the danger of a lethal outcome.

*Action:* Comply with manipulative suicidal threats.

*Result:* Submitting to "blackmail" or threats of "If you don't do this I'll kill myself" always leads to resentment and anger at the suicidal person. Therefore such compliance will eventually isolate and harm the suicidal person further. At the very least, the suicidal person has little reason to change his or her behavior and seek help in order to develop less maladaptive ways of dealing with stress; at worst, the observer will act on his or her increasing anger at the suicidal person.

*Action:* Attempt to rescue the person by yourself.

*Result:* Rescue fantasies put into action can have fatal con-

217

sequences. Even for professionals, the treatment of suicidal patients is extremely difficult; it is an impossible task for untrained family or friends. The latter can help immeasurably, but with guidance from a more objective professional. Trying to do it alone indicates a denial of the true extent of the problem. Furthermore, most people in trouble cannot speak freely about their concerns of intimates (who may themselves be part of the problem). Consequently, rescue attempts will fail, observers will feel angry and defeated, and patients will continue to think they are beyond help. Help is needed, but by trained professionals.

## Helpful Interventions

Where suicidal intent is involved, a psychiatric evaluation is necessary in order to explore fully the degree of actual risk and to initiate emergency treatment. It is better to err on the side of safety and insist on treatment early than to ignore the problem.

Some suicidal people voluntarily consent to psychiatric evaluations, particularly if they have not lost all hope. Others claim that they are being betrayed and resist all attempts at intervention. In this case, someone needs to take charge and stop the drift toward a lethal outcome. The patient should be told, "I know that you see no other way out, but I would like to help you. You may think help is foolish, since you feel you have no hope. However, this feeling of hopelessness will disappear when you get treatment for your depression." Most people will seek psychiatric care if it is suggested unambivalently in a strong and straightforward manner. If this does not convince the person to seek help, more forceful methods must be tried:

• *The police should be called* and asked to come if the danger is thought to be imminent. They can place a mental health hold on people they feel are mentally ill and a danger to themselves or others and then transport the patient to a mental health facility for further evaluation. At times the police will refuse to do this if the patient is not behaving in an obviously distraught manner.

• At the same time get help. Other friends, family, and clergy can be called for help and moral support while the patient is being transported to the doctor, hospital, or mental health center for evaluation. A show of force and concern from others may convince reticent people to become voluntary patients. Otherwise, it isn't difficult for three or four adults to force suicidal people to seek care, even if the police are unwilling to help. En route, the patient should sit in the back seat of the car between two people so he is unable to jump out or interfere with the driver. When the risk is thought to be high, the patient should not be left alone for a moment. For example: While two physicians sat on either side of a colleague, he suddenly jumped up and leaped out of a sixteenth-floor window to his death. Even if the patient has to go to the bathroom, *someone must accompany him.*

• During an active suicidal crisis there are other sources of immediate help and support. Local mental health centers have twenty-four-hour emergency services and may be contacted at any time. University and general hospitals also frequently have emergency psychiatric services that can be a source of care and advice on how to proceed. Workers from these types of agencies may be able to evaluate the patient in his home. Also, local suicide prevention centers can provide information on how to proceed.

• If the police fail to pick up the patient, mental health professionals are no help, and family and friends are unable to bring the patient for an interview, many states have another alternative: the court-ordered mental health evaluation. This should be reserved for patients who are not in immediate danger. County courts will be able to provide information on how to proceed in this direction.

If the chance of suicide is only suspected and the patient has not yet had an evaluation, there are certain things that can be done in order to judge the dangerousness of the situation.

• The patient can be asked about specific plans relating to suicide. Questions that can be asked are: "Do you have thoughts of killing yourself?" "Did you ever have such thoughts?" "What plans do you have?" "Have you made any preparations for such a plan?" If the patient admits to any plan whatsoever, an emergency exists and the actions outlined in the previous section should be taken.

• Inquiries about pills should be made and the pills located and removed. The same should be done for guns, knives, and so forth. People will be relieved by this sign of caring even if it is, at times, an overreaction.

• If a suicide attempt has already been made, the following should be asked after calling the police, ambulance, or rescue squad: "Are you glad to be alive, to have been found or have been stopped?" "What would you have done if not found or stopped?" This will be important information to give to the professional who later evaluates the patient.

• If toxic substances were ingested, call the local poison control center for instructions. If the patient is alert, attempts should be made to induce vomiting only if the patient took pills. If solvents were taken, do not follow emergency instructions on packages or bottles since they are frequently incorrect. Call poison control. Do not give the patient any stimulants or coffee. This will do no good and simply complicate the clinical picture.

• Bring the pill bottles or poison containers to the hospital with the patient. Search the patient's medicine chest, purse, and so forth, to find other pills the patient may have taken, and bring these to the hospital as well.

• If the patient has a wound and is bleeding, apply a pressure dressing. If the patient is not breathing and / or has no heartbeat, cardiopulmonary resuscitation must be initiated until help arrives. Place the patient on his / her side so that aspiration (choking) does not occur if vomiting begins.

After the medical problems are in hand, the patient must be evaluated psychiatrically before being discharged from the emergency room. This can be difficult depending on the hour of the night, the number of hours spent in the emergency room, and whether the patient feels ill or resistant. Some medical staff members may take a dim view of psychiatry. Such an evaluation *must be insisted upon,* however, before the patient leaves the hospital.

After the patient has been attended to, psychotherapeutic help for family and friends is often also indicated. It is crucial that their anxiety, guilt, and anger be recognized and dealt with. They will be less able to help the suicidal patient if they harbor unmetabolized anger and resentment. It will also be useful for family and friends to consider if things could have been done differently during the development of the suicidal crisis. Certainly, if the patient dies, grief will be complicated by an unrealistic sense of responsibility complicated by rage at the patient. The latter will often be denied. However, these complicated feelings must be acknowledged and put into perspective in order for mourning to occur.

## THE MEDICAL EVALUATION
## OF THE SUICIDAL PATIENT

Physicians encounter suicidal patients in two different situations. During the build-up phase of the suicidal crisis patients often have vague somatic complaints and signs of depression, alcoholism, or anxiety. The physician must get beyond these complaints and evaluate the patient for suicide and the other violence syndromes. The second meeting is likely to follow a suicide attempt. Patients then must be medically managed and a psychiatric consultation obtained, since most

221

physicians do not have enough experience to perform an adequate suicide evaluation or do not feel comfortable doing so.

## Commonly Made Medical Errors

The following are some of the more common medical errors that can be made with suicidal patients:

*Action:* Prescribe medication because the patient is depressed, can't sleep, or is anxious.

*Result:* Patients may complain of physical ills, a poor mood, trouble sleeping, eating, and so forth. Rarely do they say directly, "I am suicidal, I'm thinking of taking my life." Since suicide is an ambivalent act, patients usually provide ample but covert clues as to their intent. Prescribing drugs for potentially suicidal patients—while at the same time failing to do a thorough evaluation—indicates that the doctor chooses not to know what is going on.. Patients may take this as an unconscious sign that the doctor wants to be rid of them. They may act on this. Medicines such as antidepressants can be life-saving, but they should be administered with caution and only after a thorough evaluation. For example, prescriptions should be written for less than a lethal dose. If this is not possible, a family member or friend should be responsible for administering each dose.

*Action:* Do not ask the patient directly about suicidal thoughts.

*Result:* Patients sense quickly what doctors are reluctant to discuss. Though many suicidal patients feel that they are beyond help, they are relieved to find someone who cares enough to deal with intensely personal issues. The doctor's willingness to discuss suicidal thoughts may give some patients hope that things may turn out all right. If the physician does not ask, the patient may feel even more isolated and beyond help.

222

*Action:* Because of covert antipathy, handle the post-attempt suicidal patient roughly in the emergency room.

*Result:* Some medical personnel do not like suicidal patients and rough treatment is sometimes rationalized as a technique to "teach" such patients not to "make themselves sick." Suicidal patients are viewed as "creating" their own illnesses. A moral judgment is passed on their behavior. This antipathy can cause patients to be even more uncooperative and health professionals to overlook significant medical problems:

A twenty-one-year-old man was brought to the emergency room following an overdose of amphetamines. He complained of a headache and right-sided weakness but this was dismissed as "hysterical." Later it was found that the patient was having a stroke due to hypertension that was caused by the drug.

Although this is a strong example, most health professionals, including psychiatrists, are uneasy dealing with the suicidal patient.

## Helpful Medical Interventions

Patients who present the physician with symptoms and signs of stress require a thorough psychiatric evaluation, which may be done by the physician if he feels competent to do so. Otherwise, a psychiatric consultation is in order. Every attempt should be made to uncover physiological as well as psychological causes of the patient's altered mood. For example, occult carcinomas or endocrine disorders may cause a behavioral decompensation. However, patients who are depressed because of physical illness also may be suicidal.

Direct questioning is best whenever suicide is a possibility. Information should be gathered from *as many sources as possible.* Patients and families will not be insulted by the doctor's interest and usually will give truthful answers. The following

223

woman was collecting medicine for a planned overdose attempt. Only because of an internist's suspicions and direct questioning was she stopped:

A thirty-two-year-old woman came to an emergency room complaining of insomnia. The intern on duty prescribed some sleeping medicine but the senior medical resident insisted that the intern ask directly about suicidal potential. The patient admitted having suicidal thoughts and fantasies of rejoining a child who had died of leukemia one year before. This woman was seen by a psychiatric consultant, who decided to hospitalize her. She was treated successfully for a pathological grief reaction.

When suicide is suspected, the following questions are useful. Remember that homicidal thoughts often coexist with suicidal ruminations.

- "Have you ever been so upset that you thought of killing yourself?"
- "When did you have these thoughts?"
- "Do you have such thoughts now?"
- "Are you able to control yourself?"
- "Do you have a plan?"

If suicide is a possibility, a psychiatric consultation should be obtained *before* the patient leaves the office, clinic, or emergency room. Such a consultation may be obtained by telephone, if necessary, although an in-person interview is by far the preferable method for examination.

If a suicide attempt has already been made, the patient's level of lethality can be ascertained through three questions: "Were you trying to kill yourself?" "Are you surprised you survived?" "Are you glad you're alive now?" If the answer to any of these indicates either a wish to die at the time of the attempt or a continuing wish to be dead, then the patient should be considered as still highly lethal and should not be allowed to leave.

If no immediate psychiatric consultation is available, it is still wise to hospitalize patients who demonstrate continuing suicidal ideation or behavior. A mental health consultation can be obtained later. It is best to have the family agree to this, but if the physician is concerned the patient should be held in spite of the family's objections. Some families are part of the problem rather than the solution. A physician should not give undue consideration to fears of legal retribution for holding patients against their will. He is more likely to be successfully sued if he allows a patient to go who then suicides than if he involuntarily hospitalizes a patient for a short time for the patient's own safety.

## EMERGENCY PSYCHIATRIC INTERVENTIONS

By the time a suicidal person seeks out or is brought to a psychiatrist he probably feels demoralized, hopeless, and overwhelmed. His usual ways of coping have failed and he probably will view treatment as further proof of failure and another blow to his self-esteem. Therefore, a therapeutic stance of respect, hope, calm but firm questioning, and listening is essential. It is necessary to convey to the person that all is not lost and that others have respect for him even if he does not have respect for himself.

However, there are some common mistakes made during the psychiatric evaluation that will have predictable results. These can occur with patients before or following a suicide attempt.

### Commonly Made Psychiatric Errors

*Action:* Don't hospitalize the patient because of a treatment philosophy that it is "better to keep the patient in the community."

225

*Result:* Some mental health professionals view psychiatric hospitalization as a therapeutic defeat, feeling that hospitalization can be harmful and too regressive for the patient. In the acute suicidal crisis, hospitalization can be life-saving. Even if a patient's family is extremely reliable, it is a terrible burden to care for a suicidal patient in the home. Patients will sense this and will react by feeling that they are even more of a burden or are not being taken seriously by the therapist.

*Action:* Don't hospitalize the patient, because he or she does not appear deeply depressed.

*Result:* The physical and behavioral manifestations of depression do not correlate with the degree of hopelessness experienced by the patient. The latter is closely associated with lethality. Some patients who may be sleeping and eating still feel hopeless about the future. This is important to consider, too, when planning a hospital discharge for a suicidal patient. Behavioral improvement precedes cognitive change. Here again the patient may appear moderately well but remain suicidal; this intervention may lead to suicide.

*Action:* Do not interview family and friends separately or at all.

*Result:* Important information such as a recently purchased weapon can be overlooked and the full extent of the patient's difficulties not appreciated if family and friends are reticent to speak openly in front of the patient. They may be frightened of insulting the patient or of incurring his anger. Furthermore, ambivalence about the patient's behavior may be expressed by withholding important information. Therefore, it is important that these people be seen alone so that they may speak more freely. Their emotional responses to the patient should also be explored in order to uncover possible death wishes.

*Action:* Allow the suicidal patient to leave the emergency room or office without further evaluation of the potential for other violence in the patient or family.

226

*Result:* Because of ignorance or discomfort, clinicians may overlook the association of suicide with other destructive behaviors. Patients may be both suicidal and homicidal; their attacks on someone else may be an attempt to be killed themselves. In fact, suicidal behavior may be the only way some patients have of controlling homicidal impulses. In addition, suicide may be symptomatic of other family difficulties. All family members should be evaluated so that the components of the suicidal crisis will be fully understood.

## Helpful Emergency Interventions

The overriding immediate aim of any acute treatment plan is to keep the suicidal patient alive at all costs. Suicidal crises are episodic; the period of highest lethality lasts only for hours or days. Therefore, the therapeutic thrust should be to evaluate present suicidal danger or the possibility of further danger following an attempt, and how the patient will best survive the next few days. At the same time, the groundwork should be set for later psychotherapeutic efforts. Appropriate approaches outlined in the general and medical sections should be followed. In addition, psychiatric hospitalization should be considered if:

• the patient will not follow the treatment plan or feels he cannot control his suicidal impulses.
• after an interview family or friends still are concerned that the risk of suicide is high.
• after the interview the clinician is still worried even though objective evidence is lacking. Such hunches should be heeded.
• the patient lives alone or in a chaotic or unreliable situation.
• the patient falls into any of the high-risk categories.

There are two other questions that must be answered in any suicidal crisis to help judge present lethality: What was the patient trying to accomplish by suicidal behavior? and Was this accomplished? If little has been changed by the suicidal

227

activity, lethality probably remains high. This is not a minor point. For example, if an overdose is taken in order to recapture a lost love object and the patient does not achieve his goal, he may escalate the suicidal behavior. In such a case the patient can be asked what he or she thought would happen if death occurred and also about thoughts of revenge, reunion, or immortality. Queries about the exact circumstances under which the patient began having thoughts of dying or when the suicidal attempt was made also provide clues to the degree of lethality. For instance, did he or she plan to be found? and by whom?

If the patient has regained hope, is not psychotic, and will follow the treatment plan, hospitalization can be avoided. Otherwise, hospitalization will be life-saving. If the patient is to be sent home, the following steps must be taken:

• Access to weapons, pills, or other means to suicide must be restricted.
• Family and friends must be thoroughly evaluated.
• Clear plans for follow-up care should be formulated, plans that are agreeable to both patient and caretakers and that all can follow. If someone is to remain with the patient at all times, that must be clearly stated. Exact appointment times should be given for follow-up care, and plans made as to how the patient is to attend the first session.
• Addresses and telephone numbers of the patient and caretakers must be current. If the patient misses follow-up appointments, contingency plans must be made. Missing appointments can be one of the danger signals during a suicidal crisis, since this may indicate that the patient feels hopeless about the future.

The benefits of a thorough psychological evaluation cannot be underestimated. People in crisis are often confused as to what is really wrong and need the objectivity of a noninvolved therapist. During a successful evaluation, a chaotic story may become intelligible to both patient and therapist, which in itself will be beneficial. For example, a college teacher began experiencing suicidal thoughts following a visit home for the Christmas holidays. These ideas were upsetting to her and she consulted a psychiatrist because of them:

She said that she had been looking forward to this trip because she wanted to go home to be treated like a child again and to be "taken care of" for the vacation. However, when she came home things did not work out as planned and she felt "estranged" from her parents. Following this, she began having thoughts of suicide. During the initial psychiatric evaluation it became apparent that these thoughts represented suppressed rage at being forced to grow up (she was the youngest) and resentment at having to leave the home. She was no longer the "little princess" she wished to be and wanted to make her parents suffer because of this. Her suicidal preoccupations decreased in intensity as she was able to delineate their function and her underlying anger at her family.

Knowledge gives patients the opportunity to utilize less maladaptive behaviors. Self-awareness will probably make patients feel better, even though the patient's realities may remain the same.

Finally, clinicians should avail themselves of consultation from other professionals. People are rarely completely objective during emergency situations and it is well known that angry feelings about suicidal patients is not uncommon. Such consultation often helps therapists maintain the therapeutic stance necessary to deal effectively with these difficult patients.

# 7

# Psychotherapy
## SOME GUIDELINES
## AND PITFALLS

> Treatment is invisible. You may not see the changes after
> each session but I know where I've been—I know where
> I am now—and I know where I'm going.
>
> *An abusive parent*

When the initial danger has passed, people in trouble often
need psychotherapeutic help in order to avoid future crisis
situations. However, many who would most benefit from
treatment are unlikely to seek it. Psychotherapy may be misperceived as an admission of failure—of not being able to go
it alone. Some people are unsure of their ability to change.
Unsatisfactory childhood experiences also make it hard to trust
therapists later in life, particularly if parents could not be
counted on when needed. Another problem concerns the poor
sense of self usually associated with the conviction that one is
responsible for one's own difficulties; bad things are deserved
and one's problems are a just punishment. Patients, particularly those involved with dangerous behaviors, also worry that
their feelings will be translated into actions that will overwhelm themselves and others. They are, in effect, frightened
to open Pandora's box.

230

Avoidance of treatment also is avoidance of the anxiety of getting better. Even when there is a desire to alter circumstances, there is an unconscious pull in the opposite direction. For people raised by exploitive parents and taught to sacrifice themselves for parental needs, getting better may seem a betrayal of their parents. If they become less depressed and angry, happier and more autonomous, they will be resented and punished. Patients may also fear that they cannot function alone and are frightened of separating from their family. To be sick is to be dependent and cared for. To be well is to be all alone. Then there are people who resist growing up because they fear success. To succeed is felt as being too aggressive—competitive and therefore dangerous.

Others do not want to begin treatment because they anticipate the end of treatment and leaving. An attachment to anyone, in this case a therapist, evokes old feelings of depression and abandonment. Keeping therapists at a distance allows such people to distance themselves from their own internal fears of loss; enforced isolation protects against such catastrophies. Even while patients are in treatment they may have one foot out the door. For instance, one patient initially failed to note the time for his regular appointment in his schedule book. He then wrote it in pencil so that it could be "erased." Only after two years had passed did he begin writing down the appointment in ink. Because he had been neglected as a child he did not want to risk being "let down" as an adult.

Thus, the initial steps toward treatment are the hardest, the time when patients are most in need of support from family and friends. With sufficient encouragement, these people may dare to seek psychotherapy despite their conviction that such a move is potentially dangerous and will make little difference in their lives.

Finding a competent therapist, as with any physician, depends on educated luck. While it might be possible to find a very good therapist simply by consulting a telephone book, this method is risky. The safest route is to seek referrals from trusted family members, friends, or the family physician. If no recommendations are forthcoming from these sources, departments of psychiatry at medical schools or psychoanalytic institutes will offer help and referrals. Several names should be obtained, and ideally the patient should meet with a number of therapists, to see which one he or she prefers. Prospective patients should not be concerned that they might insult therapists if they shop around.

University hospital clinics or community mental health centers also provide psychiatric care with fees adjusted to the patient's financial status. In these settings patients probably will be assigned to specific therapists, but if treatment does not progress as planned, or if the therapist-patient "fit" does not seem right, patients may obtain a second opinion or transfer to a different therapist.

The initial sessions—usually one to four—are for the therapist and patient to get to know each other. There should be continuing, open discussion about the goals of treatment— what the patient wants to accomplish and whether the therapist feels this is possible within the scope of psychotherapy. Discussion about the length of treatment, the focus of treatment, fees, and billing procedures should take place early so that there are no later surprises. Questions about the therapist's training are appropriate, as well as grist for the therapeutic mill. These inquiries, although reality-based, also have emotional determinants and should be addressed on both levels. For instance, questions about the therapist's experience should be answered even if the underlying motivation is the patient's fear that the case is hopeless. Unfortunately, many patients are inhibited and do not bring up such inquiries for fear of insulting the clinician.

Each crisis presents a unique chance to rework unresolved problems—to reach a new level of understanding about one's life. During crisis, people are closer to deep and personal issues that are unavailable at calmer, more defended times. Dramatic changes are possible if the opportunity is taken. But the way in which change comes about will vary. The degree of patient improvement does not correlate with the frequency of patient visits. Nor does frequency of visits determine the intensity of the treatment. Patients who see a therapist once a week may be extremely involved and make good progress, while patients who come more often may make no moves at all.

## THERAPEUTIC TASKS

The tasks of treatment are relatively straightforward: to decrease dangerous activity, to bolster self-esteem and the ability to tolerate stress (that is, develop affect tolerance), and to lessen those feelings of humiliation, guilt, and abandonment that often precipitate maladaptive behaviors. If patients can learn to alter old, repetitive ways of doing things, thus strengthening self-regard and self-control, dangerous behavior is likely to lessen.

During the crisis state, people are often unaware of why they are upset. The sense of reality is diminished and they feel confused, overwhelmed, and disoriented. The therapeutic benefits of a thorough psychiatric examination are extremely important at this time. Through such an exam a chaotic story becomes more intelligible to the therapist and more manageable to the patient.

There are different ways to conceptualize treatment. The following outlines only one approach in which three tasks confront the patient and therapist:

- To establish the alliance
- To find the dynamic focus
- To promote adaptive responses

The various aspects of the assessment and treatment process are inseparable and occur simultaneously. However, for purposes of convenience and clarity, they have been separated here.

233

## Establishing the Alliance

During the initial phase of treatment the most important fact is that the person is *becoming a patient* and is talking to a stranger from whom he or she does not know what to expect. This issue may need to be overtly addressed. The therapist might say, "it took courage for you to come and talk to me," in order to relieve the patient of some of the anxiety inherent in seeking psychotherapy.

The best place to begin is where the patient wants to begin. If physical worries are uppermost in the patient's mind, these should be addressed first and not simply dismissed as psychosomatic. The patient will proceed at his own pace to more emotionally charged material.

The clinician should also judge in which stage of the stress response the patient finds himself. The stage of denial? The period of maladaptive behaviors? Finding out the stage of stress response for the patient's family is also important. For example, a family member may be able to appreciate the significance of certain events while the patient continues to deny that anything has happened.

Patients in crisis have a great wish to regress—to be cared for by others and to abrogate responsibility for their behavior. The major precept in any psychotherapy is to not do for patients what they can do for themselves. The ways in which the therapist does this can be subtle, such as letting patients find the right word and not supplying answers when patients are capable of arriving at their own conclusions. Patients then realize that they have the therapist's respect, and are being treated appropriately as adults.

Another way to counter regression is to ask what the patient wants to accomplish and how he or she views the problem. Psychotherapy then becomes a mutual endeavor and is emphasized as such. Questions such as, "What do you hope to accomplish in your treatment?" and "Is there anything that you expect or want me to do?" are appropriate. A depressed man who sought help after his wife left him obviously had unrealistic expectations:

At the end of the third—and ultimately, last—session the patient expressed surprise that the doctor had not called his wife to tell her to rejoin her husband. The patient expected this to happen, he said, because he had heard that this particular psychiatrist did "family therapy."

It is always important to find out what the patient wants to achieve and what he is capable of doing—not what the therapist wants the patient to accomplish. This man had hoped that the therapist would work a miracle for him. He did not understand that a therapist cannot reunite a person with someone who has left but can help the patient deal with the loss in a way that is more appropriate than, for example, threatening violence. Similarly, the psychotherapist cannot take care of a patient but can help the patient discover why he has difficulty caring for himself.

Another way of gauging patients' expectations is to ask how long they think the treatment will take. This question also reinforces the notion that patients play a part in their own treatment and reassures those patients (who need such reassurance) that treatment is not endless. At the same time, the therapist gains an understanding of the patient's defensive style. As one depressed patient said: "You mean I have a time limit? That means I will have to talk about what is on my mind!" This patient wanted treatment to last forever.

The issue of time is central to psychotherapy. Some treatments are open-ended, others are time-limited. Some psychiatrists use both approaches, depending on what the patient wants to accomplish and what the therapist thinks the patient needs. There are patients who want timeless treatments and those who want to end before they begin. The issue of the patient's and therapist's expectations should always be open for discussion. But both must realize that treatments begin in order to end (successfully). Without this realization, therapy loses its dynamic focus and becomes a series of amorphous, disconnected, and aimless chats.

Patients' cultural beliefs are an important but usually neglected aspect of psychotherapy. All people, no matter the background, have their own explanations for their difficulties—explanations that are, in part, culturally determined. The Greeks relied on humoral physiology. In our time, stress or diet is often used to account for illnesses. For some, "unconscious conflicts" justify people's behavior. Other people believe in spirits or magic or feel that a hex is responsible for their difficulties. Whatever the beliefs, they should be made explicit between therapist and patient. For example, a Chicano lawyer sought help for anxiety that he first experienced when he visited the grave of a grandparent. Only after several months of treatment did the patient tell of being "visited" by the deceased grandfather, an event that the patient felt was related to his anxiety. He thought the therapist would think him crazy and kept this important bit of history secret, even though such events are not considered unusual in the patient's culture of origin. (In fact, similar experiences are not unusual in any acute grief reaction.)

Therapists must be prepared to listen to, try to understand, and use their patient's *own* explanations for their illnesses. Otherwise, doctor and patient will not connect and the alliance will not develop. Cultural beliefs can be uncovered by asking the following:

- How do you explain your difficulties?
- How would your parents or grandparents explain them?
- What do you think would help your situation?
- What would your grandparents have found helpful?

Patients are usually more willing to speak of their relatives' beliefs than they are to acknowledge the same beliefs as their own.

236

Culture also affects treatment expectations. It is useful to remember that people regress to previous ways of thinking when they are under stress; more personal, older memories come to the surface. Nearly everyone remembers "folk" remedies from childhood. These soothing memories are likely to be recalled during adulthood in times of stress or illness. For instance, if a patient says that he was given hot tea when sick as a child, he may feel better if the doctor suggests tea with his medication. The patient certainly will be more likely to follow the doctor's prescriptions if the patient's cultural experience is taken into account. At times it may be appropriate to extend the therapeutic endeavor by referring patients to clergy or to folk healers. Confession is also therapeutically useful.

In summary, empathic listening forms the matrix in which treatment can flourish. A therapist's willingness to ask questions and to *listen* to the answers, to transmit hope and promote the idea that treatment is a cooperative effort, is the basis of the therapeutic alliance. What the patient *expects* to happen and *wants* to happen, and what the therapist *thinks* ought to happen should be openly discussed and understood.

## Finding the Dynamic Focus

It is easy to become lost in the chaotic detail of the lives of people in crisis and to overlook core psychological issues. By the time people choose to become patients, there have been many attempts and malattempts to fix whatever is wrong, and the picture can be extremely confusing. Thus, it is useful for the therapist to ask, "What happened that prompted you to pick up the phone to call me at this particular time?" "Why now?" or "What was the straw that broke the camel's back?" Patients may attempt to avoid upsetting material, but clinicians should search with patients for clues to situations of particular dynamic significance.

Most patients do not consciously understand the significance of the precipitating source of stress, even if they are able to name one. They may say that they sought help because things were "building up" or they felt "bad," or that they were involved with various dangerous behaviors "because of troubles at home." The dynamic significance of the stress that leads to maladaptive responses remains in the unconscious, and it is one task of treatment to explore the origins of these vulnerabilities.

A good therapist does not collect information in a random fashion. Rather he seeks, with the patient, to find the dynamic focus for the patient's present difficulties—to find the psychological story that runs through the patient's life. The *why now* is always related to vulnerabilities, unresolved issues in the patient's past. Past episodes of a similar nature should also be sought. It is useful to discover what evoked prior episodes, because the same issues may well be active currently. Here, again, patients may try to keep their lives compartmentalized and to avoid making connections, saying, in effect, that what happened then has nothing to do with now.

People vary in their ability to assess their own contributions as to how their lives unfold. For example, actual insults may be realistically experienced—but patients may be oblivious to their own prior provocative remarks. It is not uncommon for suicidal patients to evoke hostile and negative feeling in others, to experience these as rejections, and then to feel justified in or propelled toward suicide. Spouse abuse victims may be unclear about their involvement in destructive relationships. There is a story of a man who had a flat tire within sight of a farmhouse. He needed a wrench and set off toward the house but said to himself, "I bet that farmer has a wrench but won't want to lend it to me." He was so convinced of this that when the farmer opened the door the man said, "Goddammit, why won't you give me that wrench!" In a similar manner, many lives become self-fulfilling prophecies. People create the situations they most fear—in fact, fears often represent unconscious wishes.

Well-conducted psychotherapy—whether it is one session or many hundred—involves shifts of emphasis so that the causes of behavior are seen not as disconnected and unrelated events but as the continuing themes of a life. Psychotherapy promotes the self-observing and, therefore, healing powers of patients. The development of self-observation becomes the cutting edge for change.

Patients avoid dealing with root causes by keeping the patterns of their lives out of consciousness. Repetition serves the defensive function of protecting the person from painful history and also represents an unconscious attempt to master past trauma. It is as if the patient is saying, unconsciously, I wasn't hurt and overwhelmed then, only now. And I can fix things that happened to me long ago if I am able to master whatever present crisis I have created. Unfortunately, the past cannot be undone. For example, a young woman found herself unaccountably involved in a series of unsatisfactory relationships—one that was physically abusive, the rest emotionally unfulfilling. This woman frequently became depressed and felt worthless. The reasons for her unhappiness and the sameness of her existence remained enigmatic to her until she sought psychotherapeutic help after a severe argument with her most recent boyfriend. After a few sessions she came to the following conclusion:

"I don't want to get close to anything because I'm just going to lose it. It will go away. It will hurt you and leave. Something will happen to it. No wonder I don't let anyone close to me—look at all the pain it has caused. Begin, left, and betrayed. *I always expect it—perhaps I ask for it— maybe I deserve it—it's always there.*" (Emphasis added)

This was the theme of a life in which the patient was an active—not only a reactive—participant. She had been deserted at an early age by her mother and raised by an abusive sister. The patient did not realize that she was compulsively perpetuating and recreating her relationships with these important early figures. She was only dimly aware of her part: "Perhaps I asked for it," "Maybe I deserve it." However, by linking the past with the present—by emotionally reexperiencing and reworking buried feelings, by ultimately accepting what had happened and her responses to these events—this patient was better able to grieve the mother she never had, feel less responsible for both her mother's disappearance and her sister's misbehavior, and feel more deserving of a better life. The repetition of this theme in therapy—that the therapist, too, would desert her and let her down—made it difficult for her to enter treatment but also provided excellent material for discussion during treatment.

This case also illustrates the common experience that although connections between the past and present may be obvious to others, patients often need the help of a noninvolved person to make these associations conscious. Even then, such connections may be denied if the patient is not ready to face them. For example, this patient felt depressed every spring, the anniversary of her mother's disappearance. During the initial phases of treatment she was unable to acknowledge this connection. Only after the therapeutic alliance was solidly formed and the patient felt strong enough was she able to allow herself to see the reasons for her spring time sadness.

## Promoting the Patient's Adaptive Responses

Psychotherapists, as well as family and friends, may subscribe to the therapeutically destructive notion that they are accountable and responsible for what patients do; that it is they who must get patients to change their ways. Patients may even attempt blackmail by threats of suicide or other maladaptive behaviors. Only when clinicians free themselves from this notion can they function successfully. Otherwise, they become the patients' monitors and policemen—in a probable replay of the patients' perceptions of earlier parental relationships.

It is important to remember that it is not the therapist's job to end the patient's crisis, but to help *the patient* avoid further maladaptive responses and increase his or her own healthy maneuvers. For instance, giving advice is rarely effective—most patients will not listen. Instead, it is important to find out what options the patient thinks are possible and to support the healthiest ones. Such a method promotes patient autonomy while reducing the danger of maladaptive behaviors. It is essential to ask the patient, "What do you think you can do to make yourself feel better?" and not get into the position of saying, "I think you should do this or that."

Therapists use a number of specific techniques to help patients achieve this goal of crisis reduction. Connections between the past and present can be *interpreted*. Events, thoughts, and feelings can be *clarified* and thinking sharpened. *Environmental manipulation* involves supporting the patient's adaptive responses such as spending time with friends, hospitalization during a suicidal crisis, temporarily separating an incestuous father from the home, and so forth. The support of adaptive responses is seen in the following:

A young and abusive mother said, "Every time my boy cries I don't know what to do except to hit him." The therapist asked what else the mother could think of doing? The patient concluded that leaving the room and perhaps calling a friend as an initial strategy might be acceptable. Thus she began to introduce a delaying tactic, giving herself a chance to reflect before acting (hitting). Her ability to delay and avoid physical violence allowed the child to remain in the house while her treatment proceeded.

Another patient felt acutely suicidal following an argument with her parents:

The patient was attempting to separate herself from her very needy family and felt guilty doing so. Suicide became an escape from this dilemma and also served as a punishment for her wishes for autonomy. During earlier, similarly stressful situations, the patient successfully

241

dealt with her anxiety by resorting to physical activity—
an area in which she excelled. In a discussion with her
therapist she decided to try to go jogging and engage in
other athletic endeavors in order to see whether she
would feel better. She did, and her self-destructive
thinking decreased.

These patients were able to substitute their *own* adaptive
behaviors for other destructive maneuvers. This had at least
two benefits: danger was for the moment avoided, and these
patients felt more autonomous, adult, and in charge of their
lives.

On occasion, medication is useful in preventing maladaptive responses to stress. Medicine can be used as an adjunct to
allay anxiety, help sleep, or treat the patient's primary disorder: Antabuse for alcoholism or antidepressants for affective
disorders—for example, manic-depressive illness. Some patients do not feel well treated unless medicine is
prescribed—others are concerned about becoming dependent on pills. In either case, medication must be understood
within the context of the patient's entire treatment.

## TENSIONS IN THE THERAPEUTIC RELATIONSHIP

First he was Jesus, then a doctor,
and then a used car salesman.

*A patient describing her therapist*
*during treatment*

Normal anxieties arise when people first enter treatment.
For example: Am I yielding my independence and autonomy
to the therapist? Will I be criticized or humiliated? Will I be
found to be crazy? Am I beyond help? Can I tolerate talking
about my anxieties and misdeeds? Will I be flooded by my

feelings? Can this therapist take what I have to dish out? Is this therapist reliable?

Initially, some patients think that they must entertain their doctor, be charming, witty, bright, and engaging. They want to please—and therefore suppress negative thoughts and feelings. Some therapists may inadvertently encourage this in order to avoid hearing unpleasant material, thus reinforcing the patient's notion that they are there to care for or entertain the therapist.

Patients may withhold information in order to avoid the pain of discovery; most people believe that saying something out loud makes it more real. Minimization and rationalization serve the same function. Such statements as "He only hit me once" or "Nothing bad really happened" serve to deny the true importance of events. One patient, whose mother burned his fingers with matches after he, at age six, had started a fire, suppressed his anger and said that this punishment "seemed reasonable" since, after all, he had been naughty. As treatment progressed, he learned to be more honest in his appraisal of himself and others, having gained an empathic view of himself as a six-year-old.

It is a paradox that people enter psychotherapy to stay the same. The basic tension in treatment is that patients want to change but spend tremendous energy justifying their view of the world. They are prone to blame others for their difficulties and explain their actions as *reactions* only—not as the result of self-generated and lifelong patterns of behavior. Only when patients take some responsibility for themselves can treatment progress—a step that is often hard to take. This should not be confused with the distorted sense of guilt and responsibility experienced by many abused and neglected children.

Psychotherapy is not a linear experience. It progresses in fits and starts, and plateaus alternate with progress. Periods of seeming inactivity alternate with obvious movement. Patients may feel they are getting nowhere at the very time they are unconsciously preparing to open up new areas of inquiry and shed light on old issues. Treatment is a process of dealing repetitively with similar issues and reworking constant themes. One patient remarked, "I continue to circle the same things—but the circles seem to be getting smaller and smaller."

In the beginning of therapy the future may be bright if unrealistic: "The therapist is Jesus." Miracles are expected as well as total "cures." As treatment progresses, this attitude is replaced by a more painful appraisal of one's life and limitations. Termination may be full of sadness and anger—of early promises not kept. Old symptoms may reappear temporarily as if to indicate that not enough was accomplished. Yet change does occur and should be observable and felt in any successful treatment. As one patient, an incestuous father, said: "I no longer worry so much about failing and I am no longer so anxious. I am beginning to feel satisfied with myself."

Understanding does not change behavior automatically. People must also alter their actions voluntarily. The best example of this is found in the treatment of alcoholism, where the search for root causes frequently delays the achievement of sobriety. Understanding is always incomplete; but self-awareness allows patients to view their behavior more objectively. In a sense, to paraphrase Freud, psychotherapy allows patients to be unhappy for realistic—not neurotic—reasons. People can then make more informed choices and are less prone to take action because of unconscious factors. Life becomes fuller as a result.

## THE THERAPEUTIC RELATIONSHIP
## STRUCTURE AND DISTORTIONS

The structure of the psychotherapeutic relationship makes it possible for people to speak about their most intimate thoughts without fear that something untoward will happen. This is especially important because many patients were raised in homes where they were both overstimulated and neglected.

The psychotherapeutic environment, therefore, must be predictable in order to provide a safe arena in which treatment can take place. Patients need such structure in order to talk about "unsafe" thoughts and feelings. In a way, the therapeutic experience provides the patient with a sense of empathy and stability often lacking in the early lives of many of these patients. In this regard, well-conducted psychotherapy is based on two important principles: 1) that except for a few well-defined situations, everything that the patient brings to the treatment is confidential and 2) that feelings are to be put into words and talked about—not acted on. This is important since patients in crisis are often unsure of the limits of their own self-control, may blur the distinction between thinking and doing, and worry about being injured by others as they were in the past.

Therapist demeanor is important in calming patients' fears. Forced informality and pseudocamaraderie, making jokes or small talk—in general, turning a session into a social event—may be a pleasant diversion but is not psychotherapy. Therapists need not be stone-faced, but the time is the patient's, not the therapist's. Some therapists are unable to sustain therapeutic listening and fall under the spell of their own voices; others are unable to tolerate silences and interject their thoughts, not letting patients develop their own. Joking can become a particular problem, because jokes usually contain a core of hostility. By joking, the true intent of the communication is kept hidden, out of consciousness, and out of the treatment. For example, a patient joked that he thought he had rabies. Both he and the therapist laughed at this absurdity. Only later did it become apparent that the patient was struggling with "mad-dog" impulses. Another therapist, upon hearing that a patient needed a car, offered to sell him one. While certainly not many cars are sold in this fashion, such an offer is clearly inappropriate, since the purpose of the treatment becomes muddled: and what is the therapist going to bring up (sell) next?

The housekeeping aspects of psychotherapy—scheduling,

the uses of time, billing procedures—are all related to the therapeutic tasks at hand. Attention to these details is reassuring to most patients, since structure and routine can be soothing. Conversely, lack of organization in the therapist can create patient anxiety. Absolute precision is impossible, but because the form of the treatment is so important—it provides a psychological safety net for patients—it is helpful to begin *and* end sessions on time and bill in a timely fashion.

Time has many meanings to different people. To disorganized patients, regular and prompt appointments have a beneficial and organizing influence. Compliant patients are nearly always punctual, oppositional patients may be a few minutes late. Of course, such behavior may cover quite different emotions: the compliant patient may be hiding hostile feelings and the oppositional patient struggling against passive urges to cooperate. One patient told her therapist that "ending on time was reassuring to me in the beginning. It meant that this was a safe place to be." She had the thought that if the sessions ran overtime it meant that her therapist had a sexual interest in her. Only later in treatment was she able to explore the origin of this fantasy.

If ends of sessions are ragged, always running over, important feelings in patients may be missed. It is not uncommon for patients to feel expelled, deserted, deprived (or relieved) when time is up, but therapists who ignore the clock usually ignore these and other responses as well. A patient complained that he felt like a "schoolboy being dismissed by a headmaster" when sessions drew to a close. This would have been missed if sessions ran overtime. Another patient came late consistently—by one or two minutes—through the first year of psychotherapy, thereby reducing the length of his sessions. Eventually he said that he was angry at having to dance to the therapist's "tune" (time) and wanted the therapist to dance to his. Such important emotional responses are overlooked when the therapists engage in sloppy housekeeping. In fact, some therapists are imprecise with time because they are uncomfortable evoking these types of feelings in their patients.

The idea must be promoted that it is acceptable to bring up and discuss all feelings and behavior. However, even when this concept is voiced, therapist behavior may indicate otherwise. Therapists who indicate that certain things are off-limits inhibit what patients will deal with. Such limitations can be quite subtle. For example, a therapist may excuse a forthcoming absence (and deflect a patient's hostile feelings) by telling the patient, "I'm going on vacation . . ."—who can get angry at someone going on vacation? Doesn't everyone deserve one? One therapist displayed a typed notice on his secretary's desk: "Dr. _____ will be out of town on _____," thus implicitly stating that discussion of his absence did not belong in the treatment session. Such actions reinforce many patients' notion that one is not allowed to get angry at people upon whom one is dependent.

Patients should be given ample time to adjust to absences, vacations, or other changes in treatment, such as a change in fees. While this is not always possible, it indicates respect for patient's feelings, something that many did not experience when young. Patients may distort therapist motivations for such changes, but these are the discussions that allow patients to begin correcting their views of the world. For instance, one patient felt that her idea of herself as "defective" was confirmed by her therapist's absence. She had the fantasy that he was spending time with a "perfect" woman. When this fantasy was aired, it lost some of its power to affect the patient and provided a rich opportunity to explore her self-deprecating attitude.

Patients are not there to treat the doctor, and as a general rule, therapists should not share their personal problems with patients. For example:

A young and attractive woman, a victim of incest, was invited to enter treatment at a greatly reduced fee. Her psychiatrist told her that he found her case "particularly interesting" and that he wanted to treat patients who were "capable of insight." This was why the special financial arrangements were made. He said that since his was a practice full of "chronic and very sick" patients he did not have many patients like her.

This patient-therapist relationship became a recapitulation of the woman's earlier special and destructive relationship with her father. The patient's wish to grow up and end treatment had to be weighed against the idea that by leaving she was depriving the therapist of a particularly interesting and satisfying patient. Luckily this patient had the fortitude to seek a second opinion and was able to end this destructive, "special" therapeutic relationship.

Being special may be gratifying but also makes it difficult to talk. It is for this reason that therapists usually do not treat friends and, never, family members. If no other clinicians are available, then the former may be necessary. Yet when this happens it might indicate that the therapist has a distorted view of his self-importance. Patients in such treatments are also likely to want to impress and please a therapist they already know and may be embarrassed to talk of personal matters. Oddly enough some patients deliberately seek treatment with therapist acquaintances for just such defensive reasons.

In order to retain the boundaries of the therapeutic relationship, most clinicians do not socialize with their patients. One patient who invited her therapist to an open-house was reassured when he declined to come: "I really didn't want you to attend. And besides, if I have you as a friend, then I lose you as a doctor." She was testing the safety of the treatment.

At the same time, clinicians must be readily available during times of trouble. This privilege may be abused by certain patients who are *always* in crisis but the majority of people find the offer of availability enough. Some may test the therapist during the beginning phases of treatment. Availability is especially important in the treatment of suicidal patients because it is thought that therapists' antipathy plays a role in some successful suicides.

## Distortions in the Therapeutic Relationship

A number of problems can occur in the therapist-patient relationship. Trouble arises when therapists, either because of lack of training or unconscious factors, begin to fulfill or exploit their patients' neurotic wishes, or act in other ways that are destructive to treatment. Most therapists guard against using patients and are largely successful in this endeavor. They utilize supervision, consultation with colleagues, and their own personal treatments to help in this regard. Some therapists, those who are poorly trained or poorly suited to the profession, may have a harder time not capitulating to their own wishes to be admired, loved, or needed. Problems arise more often for these therapists when dealing with the overstimulating and highly anxiety-producing material commonly associated with dangerous behaviors.

Most people choose careers for intensely personal reasons—adult choices of profession often reflect attempts to deal with childhood issues, and therapists are no exception. Some people become psychotherapists because they were compelled to care for and be responsible for their own parents—in fantasy or reality—when they were young. Such clinicians continue to carry out imagined obligations as adults. If patients do not respond to treatment, these clinicians may get angry because they reexperience the helplessness and guilt they felt in childhood. It is not by chance that some child protection workers experienced neglect when young, or that some therapists involved with the treatment of incest or spousal violence have personal acquaintance with these problems. Other therapists want to be part of other people's lives—to be intimate at a distance—since they felt isolated as children. Patients run the risk of becoming unconscious stand-ins for parents—

249

or therapists may treat patients as if they were themselves. In either case, therapeutic objectivity is lost. In essence, the patient is asked to treat the therapist.

Exploitation can take many forms. Sometimes therapists underestimate what patients can do; at other times, patients are expected to accomplish too much. To burden patients with the therapist's expectations gives patients a task at which they will fail. It creates a situation where the patient is being asked to get better for the therapist—to treat the therapist's professional self-esteem. If the therapeutic environment becomes unpredictable and therapists use their patients for themselves, boundaries become indistinct and patients' self-control is undermined. At best, treatment will fail, but it is more likely that problems will be inflamed.

Two distortions of the therapeutic relationship require special mention: breaches of confidentiality and sexual acting out with patients. Both involve breaking the two central rules of psychotherapy: that except for a few well-defined situations, everything the patient brings to treatment is confidential, and feelings are to be put into words and talked about, not acted on. Action, especially aggressive or erotic behavior by either the patient or therapist, is unacceptable.

## Confidentiality

Confidentiality is the patient's, not the therapist's, privilege. The patient can speak to others about the treatment but the clinician should say nothing. If a patient is hospitalized, the fact of hospitalization should be kept confidential unless *the patient* gives permission to do otherwise. If a friend or family member calls the hospital, no information should be given— not even that the patient is receiving psychiatric care. If the patient wants others to know, the patient, not the hospital or clinician, should be the informant.

There are some exceptions. Maladaptive behaviors precipitate situations where confidentiality may have to be broken. When danger is suspected it is frequently necessary for the therapist to contact family and friends in order to gather information or to inform them of the therapist's concerns. But patients should be given the opportunity to consent to such contacts. If they don't agree, the clinician must decide if the danger overrides the privilege. In certain situations, child abuse for example, there is no choice, and the abuse must be reported to the local authority. But even then patients should be told why confidentiality is being broken.

Some therapists, when anxious, may gossip. Instead of reflecting why tensions exist, therapists sometimes act and talk in an attempt to allay anxiety. This may be a particular problem when patients are dealing with the kind of intense, frightening, or overstimulating material common to dangerous behaviors. Gossiping also builds self-esteem at the expense of others. Being "in the know" gives a certain stature to the bearer of information. Gossip usually involves information about the humiliations or misfortunes of others—another way of putting them down. The impulse to gossip, then, is a clue for the therapist to seek consultation or engage in self-examination.

There are other pressures that weaken confidentiality. Institutions, insurance companies, hospitals and staff of health planning organizations often have access to information. In some minds, needs for information outweigh patients' rights to privacy. Charts are often left lying around for anyone to see in record rooms of hospitals or other institutions. Insurance forms can be reviewed by a number of clerks. Therefore, a therapist should remember that all information written down is likely to be seen by many eyes, and act accordingly.

## Sexual Exploitation

Much publicity has been given to the issue of sexual activity between patients and therapists. Physicians and other therapists are against such behavior, but it appears to be an old problem, since the Hippocratic oath specifically warns against such practices. There are no situations where such behavior is beneficial for the patient. In fact, this behavior usually involves the patient's acting out—once again—self-destructive behaviors and the therapist's exploitation of the patient's dependent position.

Patients unconsciously try to recreate aspects of old traumas in new relationships. The advantage of being in psychotherapy is that patients can become aware of these urges. When fantasies can be put into words, the patient has a chance not to repeat endlessly. However, if fantasies are acted upon, they remain unconscious and the treatment relationship becomes like all others. The problem of repetition is especially acute with victims of sexual abuse if these victims are seductive even while not being aware of such behavior. To be sexual is, for many, to be loved. When therapists respond rather than reflect—or actually attempt to seduce—they are betraying a patient as the patient's parents did before them. It is the author's impression that the majority of patients who have sex with their therapists were abused, sexually, physically, or emotionally, when they were young.

Some therapists offer elaborate rationalizations for their sexual behavior, claiming that patients are helped by such activity. Yet, these explanations belie their neurotic underpinnings. For instance:

A male clinician began treating a young woman—an adult victim of childhood incest. As is common, the patient developed intense feelings about her therapist. The therapist moved from town four years after the treatment began, but the patient continued corresponding with him. When he returned, they began dating. He felt this was all right since they were "no longer doctor and patient."

This doctor was reenacting the patient's earlier experiences. Patients have every right to express *any* fantasy they wish, but therapists—like parents with their children—have no right to take up their patients' offers. Some may argue that acting in these ways can be corrective and curative. Yet, such behavior will always have the unconscious meaning of being illicit and exploitive—it will always mean the betrayal of therapeutic trust.

The therapist never entirely loses the aura and responsibilities of healer, and rarely does the patient completely resolve the complex feelings toward the therapist that were generated during psychotherapy. As another patient who had an affair with her ex-therapist, said: "I feel absorbed by other people's needs. I lose sight of who I am. I am important only in terms of what others want from me." Her therapist, rather than helping her to change this self-view, took advantage of it a few years after treatment had ceased. Once a patient, always a patient, even though treatment may have been terminated many years before.

## OBTAINING A SECOND OPINION

Patients and therapists should continuously question the usefulness of treatment. How is it progressing? What core dynamic problems have been identified? Are the issues becoming clearer, if more painful? Are misperceptions about oneself that once were tenaciously clung to giving way to more positive self-esteem? Has there been an increase in feelings of mastery and a decrease in maladaptive behaviors? Does the patient have the feeling that the therapist is trying to help and understand even if the help is not always felt to be enough and the understanding incomplete? Negative answers should precipitate a reevaluation of the utility of the therapeutic relationship. Some patients fail to get better despite the care they receive. Sometimes this has to do with the "fit" between therapist and patient or to other variables as yet unspecified. At times like these, a second look is also helpful.

A consultation should be sought (by either the patient or clinician) when treatment seems not to be going well, if the patient feels there is no progress, or if the symptoms are getting worse with no adequate therapeutic explanation such as working with difficult or upsetting material. Patients may feel stuck in one place for too long or think that the therapist's view of their problems is incongruent with their own. Patients may also feel that their therapist is too critical or gives too much advice. There may be other complaints. These feelings may result from patient distortions, yet therapists, too, may be responsible.

Second opinions, commonly obtained in other branches of medicine, are relatively rare in psychiatry. Yet such consultations, when handled properly, can benefit both therapist and patient. A noninvolved clinician can shed light on treatment impasses and often such consultations allow treatments to gain new vigor. Clinicians who will provide a second opinion can be found in the same way as was the original therapist: through friends, physicians, university departments, or from the original therapist.

It is not clear why people get better; not clear what the therapeutic agents in psychotherapy really are. But people do get better. The confessional aspects of psychotherapy should not be underestimated. Self-understanding and feeling understood and not criticized are important, as are imitation and unconscious identification with the therapist's introspective and reasoned ways of looking at things. The enhancement of self-observing functions certainly occurs along with self-understanding. People carry away from psychotherapy a different way of looking at things and then, it is hoped, of doing things.

When a patient (or family) is committed to change, change will occur. Many people involved in dangerous behaviors do not know any other way to act when they are under stress. The psychotherapist and therapeutic environment provide the arena in which these people can explore, in safety, the repetitive nature of their history. They may then find they do have a choice and are not compelled to repeat and re-experience the distortions of the past.

254

# Bibliography

## Chapter 1: THE MALADAPTIVE RESPONSE

Caplan, Gerald. "Mastery of Stress: Psychosocial Aspects," *American Journal of Psychiatry* 138 (1981):413–20.

Dalton, K. "Cyclical Criminal Acts in Premenstrual Syndrome," *Lancet* 2 (1980):1070–71.

Dubovsky, Steven L., and Weissberg, Michael P. *Clinical Psychiatry in Primary Care.* 2nd edition. Baltimore: Williams and Wilkins, 1982.

Elliott, Frank A. "The Neurology of Explosive Rage," *The Practitioner* 217 (1976):51–60.

Goldstein, Murray. "Brain Research and Violent Behavior," *Archives of Neurology* 30 (1974):1 35.

Holinger, P. C. "Violent Deaths Among the Young: Recent Trends in Suicide, Homicide, and Accidents," *American Journal of Psychiatry* 136 (1979):1144–47.

Horowitz, Mardi. "The Stress Response Syndrome," *Archives of General Psychiatry* 31 (1974):768–81.

Reite, Martin, and Caine, Nancy. *Child Abuse: The Nonhuman Primate Data.* New York: Alan R. Liss, in press.

Sadoff, R. L. "Violence in Families," *The Bulletin of the American Academy of Psychiatry and the Law* 4 (1976):292–96.

Shengold, Leonard. "The Effects of Overstimulation: Rat People," *International Journal of Psychoanalysis* 48 (1967):403–15.

## Chapter 2:   ALCOHOLISM

Bean, M. "Identifying and Managing Alcohol Problems of Adolescents," *Psychosomatics* 23 (1982):389–96.

Crowley, Thomas J., and Rhine, Mark W. "Abuse of Alcohol and Other Drugs," in *Understanding Human Behavior in Health and Illness.* Richard C. Simons, M.D., and Herbert Pardes, M.D., eds. Baltimore: Williams and Wilkins, 1981.

Dilts, Stephen L. "Substance Abuse," in *Clinical Psychiatry in Primary Care.* Steven L. Dubovsky, M.D., and Michael P. Weissberg, M.D., eds. 2nd edition. Baltimore: Williams and Wilkins, 1982.

Seixas, F. A. "Alcoholism Treatment: A Descriptive Guide," *Psychiatric Annals* 12 (1982):375–85.

## Chapter 3:   CHILD ABUSE

Kempe, C. H., and Helfer, R. E., eds. Helping the Battered Child and His Family. Philadelphia: J. B. Lippincott, 1972.

Kempe, C. H. *The Battered Child.* 3rd edition. Chicago: University of Chicago Press, 1980.

Martin, H. *The Abused Child: A Multidisciplinary Approach to Developmental Issues in Treatment.* Cambridge, MA: Ballinger Press, 1976.

Schmitt, Barton D., ed. *The Child Protection Team Handbook.* New York: Garland Press, 1978.

Schmitt, B. D.; Bross, D. E.; Carroll, C. A.; et al. Guidelines for the Hospital and Clinic Management of Child Abuse and Neglect, DHEW Publication No. (OHDS) 79, 30167, August 1978.

Steele, B. F. "Working with Abusive Parents from a Psychiatric Point of View." DHEW Publication No. (OHD), 1975.

Weissberg, M. P. "The Somatic Complaint: A Ticket of Admission for Child Abusers," *Primary Care* 4 (1977):283–89.

Winnicott, D. W. "Mirror-role of Mother and Family in Child Development," in *The Predicament of the Family.* P. Lomas, ed., Pp. 26–33. London: Hogarth Press, 1972.

## Chapter 4:   FATHER-DAUGHTER INCEST

Herman, J., and Hirschman, L. "Families at Risk for Father-Daughter Incest," *American Journal of Psychiatry* 138 (1981):967–70.

McCaghy, C. H. "Child Mothering," *Sex Behavior* 1 (1971):16–24.

Meiselman, K. C. *Incest: A Psychological Study of Causes and Effects with Treatment Recommendations.* San Francisco: Jossey-Bass, 1978.

Nakashima, I. I., and Zakus, G. "Incestuous Families," *Pediatric Annals* 8 (1979):29–42.
"Child Sexual Abuse: Incest, Assault and Sexual Exploitation." DHEW Publication No. (OHDS) 79, 30166, 1979.


Chapter 5:  SPOUSE ABUSE

Hilberman, E. "Overview: The 'Wife-Beater's Wife' Reconsidered," *American Journal of Psychiatry* 137 (1980):1336–47.
Steinmetz, Suzanne K., and Straus, Murray A., eds. *Violence in the Family*. New York: Harper and Row, 1974.
Wolfgang, M. E. "Family Violence and Criminal Behavior," *Bulletin of the American Academy of Psychiatry and the Law* 4 (1976):316–27.


Chapter 6:  SUICIDE

Maltzburger, John T., and Buie, Dan H. "Countertransference Hate in the Treatment of Suicidal Patients," *Archives of General Psychiatry* 30 (1974):625–33.
Miles, C. P. "Conditions Predisposing to Suicide: A Review," *The Journal of Nervous and Mental Disease* 164 (1977):231–46.
Murphy, G. E. "The Physicians Responsibility for Suicide, I and II," *Annals of Internal Medicine* 82 (1975):301–9.
Rosenbaum, Milton, and Richman, Joseph. "Suicide: The Role of Hostility and Death Wishes from the Family and Significant Others," *American Journal of Psychiatry* 126 (1970):1652–55.


Chapter 7:  PSYCHOTHERAPY

Frances, A., and Clarkin, J. F. "No Treatment as the Prescription of Choice," *Archives of General Psychiatry* 38 (1981):542–45.
Karasu, T. B. "The Ethics of Psychotherapy," *American Journal of Psychiatry* 137 (1980):1502–12.
Kardener, S. H.; Fuller, M.; Mensh, I. N. "A Survey of Physicians Attitudes and Practices Regarding Erotic and Nonerotic Contact with Patients," *American Journal of Psychiatry* 130 (1973):1077–81.
Malan, D. H. *Frontiers of Brief Psychotherapy*. New York: Plenum, 1976.
Mann, T. *Time-Limited Psychotherapy*. Cambridge, MA: Harvard University Press, 1973.

Miller, Alice. "The Drama of the Gifted Child and the Psychoanalyst's Narcissistic Disturbance," *International Journal of Psychoanalysis* 60, Part I (1979):47–58.

Warner, R., and Weissberg, M. "The Assessment of Psychiatric Emergencies," in *Practice and Management of Psychiatric Emergency Care.* J. Gorton and R. Partridge, eds. St. Louis: Mosby, in press.

# Index

259

# INDEX